TRANSITIONING
FROM FAMINE TO
Fruitfulness

A 30-Day Journey
Into Fresh Hope

BRENDA FINK

Cover photo credit: Photodune

Proofreader: Donna Scuderi

Layout & Design:
Tarsha L. Campbell

Published by:
DOMINIONHOUSE Publishing & Design, LLC
P.O. Box 681938 | Orlando, Florida 32868 | 407.703.4800
www.mydominionhouse.com

The Lord gave the Word: great was the company
of those who published it. (Psalms 68:11)

Acknowledgments

I would like to thank my father, James, for encouraging me to follow my dream of writing, and my mother, Helen, for patiently listening as I read my stories and poems to her.

I would like to thank my pastors, Bishop Mark Chironna and Pastor Ruth Chironna, for their faithful sowing of the Word of God into my life and their encouragement to pursue my destiny.

Finally, I would like to thank my friends who believe in me, allow me to bounce ideas around with them, and continually encourage me to share my writing.

Behold, the eye of the LORD is on those

who fear Him, on those who hope in His

mercy, to deliver their soul from death,

and to keep them alive in famine.

Our soul waits for the LORD;

He is our help and our shield. For our

heart shall rejoice in Him, because we have

trusted in His holy name.

Let Your mercy, O LORD, be upon us,

just as we hope in You.

~(Psalms 33:18-22, NKJV)

TABLE OF CONTENTS

Introduction 9

Day 1
Days of Famine 13

Day 2
Natural Sight vs. Spiritual Insight 19

Day 3
Dry and Thirsty Land 25

Day 4
Fear-Based Thinking 31

Day 5
Wheat and Tares 39

Day 6
Misplaced Hope 45

Day 7
Lost Hope 51

Day 8
Surrounded by Bad News 57

Day 9
A Word Behind You 63

Day 10
Unconditional Love 69

Day 11
Excess Baggage 75

TABLE OF CONTENTS

Day 12
The Question of Intention. **81**

Day 13
Friendship and Bitterness **89**

Day 14
A Heart of Bitterness. **95**

Day 15
Finding Fulfillment **101**

Day 16
Looking for Favor **107**

Day 17
Advice from a Wise Counselor **113**

Day 18
Why Me? **119**

Day 19
Feeding on Overflow. **125**

Day 20
Where Will Favor Take You? **131**

Day 21
Who Are You—Really? **139**

Day 22
Six Measures of Barley. **147**

Day 23
Be Still. **153**

TABLE OF CONTENTS

Day 24
Spoken Blessings 161

Day 25
What Hope Needs .167

Day 26
Naomi's Restoration 173

Day 27
What's in the Family Line? 179

Day 28
Birthing Worship. .187

Day 29
Where Will Worship Carry You? 195

Day 30
Make Room for a King 203

Meet the Author .210

Contact the Author 211

More from the Author 212

"Here in this shriveling economy are two people who are watching the dwindling resources of their neighbors and friends, and indeed the decline of their nation and are wondering how long before it touches their door. Here in the fading light of God's smile, hope is challenged and destinies are changed."

INTRODUCTION

T he book of Ruth pulls back the curtain on Hebrew culture to give a glimpse of one family living in the town of Bethlehem, in the region known as Judah, during the time when a famine was in the land. We are told in the beginning of this biblical account, the events occurred during the time when judges were ruling the nation of Israel. The Jewish historian, Josephus, suggests the time frame was during the time Eli was high priest of the land because there was a famine during his tenure.

After the death of Joshua there was no single unifying leader heading the nation so the people of Israel fell into disunity. Even though God had set in place men of authority to guide them the scripture says in Judges 17:6, *"In those days there was no king in Israel; everyone did what was right in his own eyes."*

Since there was no unifying leader, the people of Israel soon fell into bondage to the remaining nations that surrounded them in the Promised Land. Even though they had been commanded to do so, the Israelites had not fully conquered the land of Canaan given to them by God, and had not fully expelled the former inhabitants.

God raised up judges to act as deliverers to the people, and while there were some stunning victories, the Israelites chose instead to make alliances with some of the remaining people groups and eventually began to accept their gods and their worship as their own. Because of their willful disobedience to the laws and commands given to Israel through Moses, God withdrew His presence for a season from His beloved people and allowed a famine to overtake the land. While the intimacy of His presence was not overshadowing them, the depth of His love for them remained. His plan was one of redemption, expecting that the physical hunger of the people would be a guide to lead them back to a place of spiritual hunger for His friendship once again.

This is the backdrop to the book of Ruth. They were living in a time where the reality of the famine affected every person in the nation of Judah—literally every realm of the socio-economic sphere was touched by the drought that led to crop failure and food shortages.

Here in this barren land where God temporarily chose to step outside of the daily lives of His children, reside a husband and wife named Elimelech and Naomi. Here in this shriveling economy are two people who are watching the dwindling resources of their neighbors and friends, and indeed the decline of their nation and are wondering how long before it touches their door. Here in the fading light of God's smile, hope is challenged and destinies are changed.

While many of us have never experienced a famine in the natural, we all have been touched at some level by a famine of the soul. Spiritual famine may come to each person differently, but all have the same basic component—our faith is attacked, our hope fades, and we feel overwhelmed by despair, fear, and anger. We begin to doubt who we are in Christ and whether our God has the power (or the desire) to save us. We feel powerless to affect the change necessary to break the cycle of despair and move forward in life.

Famines that find their way into the heart start with fading vision. As vision fades, our strength of hope also begins to fade. Fading hope will cause us to disconnect from our internal seed of hope placed by God within every person, and ultimately will pull us away from the bright future God has for us.

As we move through the story of Ruth, we will look at how famine affected each character, some in positive ways and some in negative ways. Some in the story could not move past their own soul-famine, while others used it to spur them on to the great things God had in store for them. As you read through each day, I encourage you to allow the Holy Spirit to guide you to places in your own heart where the seeds of spiritual famine have taken root. As you spend time mediating and listening to the Holy Spirit, He will lead you out of famine into a place of fruitfulness where abundance and great joy are your reward.

"Ask the Holy Spirit to pour down His rain of healing presence and wholeness on you now and give Him permission to wash away those things that are keeping you from all He has for you."

DAY
1

DAYS OF FAMINE

Now it came to pass, in the days when the judges ruled, that there was a famine in the land. And a certain man of Bethlehem, Judah, went to dwell in the country of Moab, he and his wife and his two sons.

~(Ruth 1:1-2, NKJV)

Famine is a driving force. The famine that was sweeping across the land drove Elimelech and his family away from their home. Famine in the spiritual realm can drive us into unbelief and lives of separation from the Father.

Elimelech did what comes so easy to most of us, and probably what we would do given similar circumstances. He took his eyes off of God. He seemed to be relying only on what his natural eye was telling him, allowing fear of what could happen if the famine continued to worsen to cloud his thinking and plant seeds of mistrust in God's faithful provision.

Today we are not facing a natural famine as they did in Judah–instead, we face a famine of hope. In today's society we watch mortgage and interest rates, stock forecasts and home sales, while gleaning our sense of safety and well-being from the nightly news reports. These may be good sources of information, but they were never intended to be the sole guide in our decision making process. As believers we can glean a more sure guidance through the Word of God and the leading of the Holy Spirit.

So, how do you live strong in a climate of fear? We do exactly what the people of Judah were doing in their day. We pray for rain.

Rain in the natural is vital to crop development and future economic stability. Rain in the spiritual realm is vital to wholeness of body, soul and spirit. Ask the Holy Spirit to pour down His rain of healing presence and wholeness on you now and give Him permission to wash away those things that are keeping you from all He has for you.

QUIET REFLECTIONS _____

Are you experiencing a famine of hope right now? If so, ask the Holy Spirit to show you the things that brought you to this place. Was it circumstances? Attitudes of the heart, or long-held beliefs? Unforgiveness, or regret?

_____ **PRAYER TIME**

Holy Spirit, as I open my heart to You now, I ask that You cleanse my heart of unbelief and mistrust in my heavenly Father and His goodness. Father, I ask that You replant Your seed of hope in my heart and water it now with the rain of Your presence. I thank You for all Your benefits and Your faithfulness to me and I bless what you are doing in my life. Amen.

My Personal Reflections

_____

_____

_____

_____

_____

_____

_____

_____

_____

_____

_____

_____

_____

_____

_____

_____

_____

_____

My God Speaks

_____

_____

_____

_____

_____

_____

_____

_____

_____

_____

_____

_____

_____

_____

_____

_____

_____

_____

"How often do we do the same thing

Elimelech did? We look at what we have in

our hands and say it is less than I need and

I can't see anything better coming on the

horizon. Then we end up naming our gift

for the future as lack, insufficiency,

or even failure."

DAY

2

NATURAL SIGHT VS. SPIRITUAL INSIGHT

*The name of the man was Elimelech, the name of his wife
was Naomi, and the names of his two sons were Mahlon and
Chilion—Ephrathites of Bethlehem, Judah. And they went
to the country of Moab and remained there.*

~(Ruth 1:2, NKJV)

You've most likely heard the saying before that seeing is
believing. It actually goes much deeper than that. Our
ability to see into the spiritual realm affects who we are
at the core of our being. We establish our core beliefs on what
we see with both our natural eyes and the eyes of our heart. And
our core beliefs make us who we are.

Elimelech relied on what he was seeing with his natural eyes
when he made his decision to leave Bethlehem. In the dry
barrenness of his homeland, his vision for the future began to
wane. As his vision faded, the strength of his hope also began to
fade. So great was the decline of his heart that it eventually led

him to a place of disconnection from his internal seed of hope placed by God within every man, and ultimately pulled him away from the land of promise into a land of broken promises and failure. He moved away from a famine in the natural realm only to end up in a far worse famine of the spirit.

We catch a glimpse of what Elimelech believed about the possibilities for the future in the names he chose for his sons. His hope for a better life had so faded away, and with it his ability to see a brighter future for his children, that he names them based on the desolation he is seeing with his natural eyes. His first son he names Mahlon, which means "sickness." His second son he names Chilion, which means "wasting away."

How often do we do the same thing Elimelech did? We look at what we have in our hands and say, "It is less than I need and I can't see anything better coming on the horizon." Then we end up naming our gift for the future as lack, insufficiency, or even failure. God gave the gift of two sons and with them, hope for a future and a legacy, but Elimelech had vision only for what was immediately around him. He quickly declared his future to be filled with sickness and wasting away.

The Bible says in Proverbs, "If people can't see what God is doing, they stumble all over themselves; but when they attend to what he reveals, they are most blessed" (Proverbs 29:18, THE MESSAGE Bible). When we come to a place in our heart where we only see Him and not our circumstances, we will bear fruit in every atmosphere and every season.

QUIET REFLECTIONS _____

Faith feeds vision. Vision feeds imagination. Imagination feeds hope. What are you feeding on? What gift has God given you for your future? What are you naming the things God has given you? Do you recognize it as something you can work with and build on, or as too small and insignificant for the dream you carry?

_____ **PRAYER TIME**

Heavenly Father, I thank You that You are opening the eyes of my heart and causing me to see every gift You place in my hand as good. I decree and declare that my season of lack is over and I am moving into a season of abundance in every spiritual gift from heavenly places. I thank You for Your great love for me and I bless what You are doing in my life. Amen.

My Personal Reflections

My God Speaks

_____

_____

_____

_____

_____

_____

_____

_____

_____

_____

_____

_____

_____

_____

_____

_____

_____

_____

_____

"When we choose to see ourselves as less than what He says we are, we devalue His Word in our lives and cut ourselves off from His plan and purpose. Believing what God says about us is always more important than believing what others say about us."

DAY
3

DRY AND THIRSTY LAND

O God, You are my God; early will I seek You; my soul thirsts for You; my flesh longs for You in a dry and thirsty land where there is no water.

~(Psalms 63:1, NKJV)

Famine brings with it a host of other challenges. The continued lack of rain carried Elimelech and his family into a prolonged season of dwindling supplies, decreasing financial security, and declining emotional stability.

The lack of rain brought the loss of existing crops, as well as the loss of seed to plant in the next season. Livestock couldn't be fed, and vineyards couldn't be maintained. The very things the people were used to feeding on were slowly being taken from them and there was nothing they could do about it.

Crop failures progressed into a loss of money, which turned into financial distress and disaster for many. Financial issues led to a loss of status among peers and community leaders. The loss of status led to a loss of relationships, which brought them into a loss of connectedness. And a loss of connection with others ultimately leads to a loss of identity.

Oftentimes we find our identity in what we possess instead of our relationship with the Father. Our status in society is based on our income, the people we know, and in what circles we travel socially. This was not the case for Jesus. He didn't have to "figure out" who He was or what He was called to do. He found His identity in the voice of His Father's affirmation and approval. (See Luke 3:22).

As believers we likewise find our identity in how the Father sees us. In His eyes we are His beloved, the apple of His eye, His very likeness on the earth, His chosen ones, kings and priests, and joint-heirs with Jesus. When we choose to see ourselves as less than what He says we are, we devalue His Word in our lives and cut ourselves off from His plan and purpose. Believing what God says about us is always more important than believing what others say about us.

QUIET REFLECTIONS _____

In the garden God established the identity of man when He said, "Let Us make man in Our image and Our likeness." Then He established the purpose of man—let them have dominion. Identity comes before purpose. Who you are will always be more important than what you do. How do you define yourself? What affirmations have been spoken over you by others? How do you identify yourself? Is it based on what you hear the Father saying about you, or based on what you do?

_____ **PRAYER TIME**

Father, I thank You that You speak words of life and affirmation over me continually. I choose this day to find my identity in who You say I am. Cleanse my heart of negative words spoken about me and let Your good words take root instead. As I search out the Scriptures, open my eyes more and more to who You say I am. I love You, Lord, and I bless what You are doing in my life. Amen.

My Personal Reflections

My God Speaks

_____

_____

_____

_____

_____

_____

_____

_____

_____

_____

_____

_____

_____

_____

_____

_____

_____

_____

"What do you do when you find yourself in a season of change you didn't bargain for? In Elimelech's case, he turned and ran. Perhaps he believed he could outrun God's judgment on the land by moving away, but in doing so he cut himself and his family off from God's mercy."

DAY
4

FEAR-BASED THINKING

And they went to the country of Moab and remained there.

~(Ruth 1:2b, NKJV)

Let's take a brief look at the history of Moab, a neighboring country to Israel. After God miraculously delivered Lot, the nephew of Abraham, out of the land of Sodom, his daughters became filled with fear that they would never be able to marry and continue the family lineage. Their fear led them to carry out a devious plan to accomplish their goal. Since they had no brothers, they believed they should take it upon themselves to produce children and carry on the family name. They made the decision to get their father drunk and each in turn laid with him. Ammon and Moab were the sons born from this unholy union.

These sons grew to become the fathers of two nations bordering the land of Israel. Lot's incestuous relationship with his daughters began the history of failed fatherhood that plagued the nations of Moab and Ammon. Both nations had at the root of their worship a system of gods and idolatry that led the people away from the worship of the God of Israel.

Elimelech exposed his family to the false gods and idolatrous worship of Moab when they took up residence within its borders. He pulled himself and his family away from a place where God's judgment was tempered by His mercy and into a place where God was not worshiped or honored in any way.

What do you do when you find yourself in a season of change you didn't bargain for? In Elimelech's case, he turned and ran. Perhaps he believed he could outrun God's judgment on the land by moving away, but in doing so he cut himself and his family off from God's mercy.

We think we are escaping our problems when we turn and run when instead, we are moving ourselves further and further away from God's promise of provision and safekeeping. When we step outside the covering of His promises we are left to "make it happen" by ourselves. Restlessness increases and we enter survival mode, busying ourselves with what we need to make it through another day.

Decisions made out of fear are not rooted in divine guidance. Living in survival mode is to live with a fear-based mentality.

Perhaps the saddest phrase in this scripture is not so much that they moved to Moab, but that they remained there. Ultimately, the fear-based decision to move cost Elimelech his life and the lives of his two sons.

How can we break a fear-based mentality? First of all, we need to own our fear. Recognizing and acknowledging that our thoughts are fear-based weakens its power over us. Secondly, recognize what God has already given us—a spirit of power, love, and a sound mind. (See 2 Timothy 1:7). As believers we have access to the mind of Christ and we are admonished in the Word to let His mind be our own. May we let our thoughts and the conclusions we draw from them be influenced by His thoughts!

QUIET REFLECTIONS _____

David was faced with the opportunity to run away from his challenges or run toward them on numerous occasions. While in the field watching over his father's sheep, he would encounter wild animals. Each time he chose to face down his fear and each time he conquered what was facing him. With each victory came an increase of faith and a greater understanding of the One in whom he believed. (See 1 Samuel 17).

What are the decisions you allowed yourself to make that are based in fear? What are the challenges you are facing in your life right now? Are you running from them, or toward them in victory?

_____ **PRAYER TIME**

Father I thank You that I am not fatherless, but I am loved and accepted by You as much as You love and accept Jesus. Open my eyes to see more clearly who You are, and who I am in You. Show me the places where I am making decisions based in fear and not in faith. Break the power of fear in my life. Holy Spirit, reveal to me the mind of Christ and grant me the strength and the wisdom to walk in faith, regardless of the circumstances happening around me. I love You, Lord, and honor You as my King. I bless what You are doing in my life. Amen.

YOUR FOOD FOR THOUGHT MOMENT

You most likely recall the story of the man known as the Crocodile Hunter, Steve Irwin, who died suddenly in a shocking accident with a stingray in September 2006. The stingray has venomous stingers on its tail, which it uses as weapons of self-defense.

Much like the stingray, fear will strike our heart when our way of thinking, believing, or being is threatened in some way. Our heart uses fear as a self-defense mechanism to prevent us from making changes.

If someone were to ask you now to fill in the blank, how would you complete the statement, "Change is _____."

Did you answer, "Change is hard"? It's a common answer. It's much easier to believe that change is hard than to believe that change is necessary to move forward.

Fear can be subtle in the way it influences our decision making. Fear will continually blindside our decision making processes until we can see it for what it really is and how we have allowed it to influence us.

Allow me to encourage you in this area. Don't be afraid of your fear! Instead, learn how to feel it and then move past it.

My Personal Reflections

_____

_____

_____

_____

_____

_____

_____

_____

_____

_____

_____

_____

_____

_____

_____

_____

_____

_____

My God Speaks

_____

_____

_____

_____

_____

_____

_____

_____

_____

_____

_____

_____

_____

_____

_____

_____

"There is a season of refining that God brings to burn off those things we've allowed to take root. It is the fire of His boundless love. The burning comes when a level of maturity is reached and the strength of the seed we have taken in is such that it can withstand the crucible of truth."

DAY
5

WHEAT AND TARES

But who can endure the day of His coming? And who can stand when He appears? For He is like a refiner's fire and like launderers' soap. He will sit as a refiner and a purifier of silver; He will purify the sons of Levi, and purge them as gold and silver, that they may offer to the LORD an offering in righteousness.

~(Malachi 3:2-3)

Elimelech thought he was doing the right thing by moving away from the famine in Bethlehem. To him, he was keeping hope alive by not selling off his property, believing that one day he and his family would return home. In reality, he was mixing the seed of hope with the seed of fear.

The seed of hope is represented by the keeping of his land, which meant he would maintain at least some of his status in the community. The seed of fear is represented by the choice to move away into a land where God was not honored.

Hope and fear are frequently joined together. It's the wheat and the tares growing together in the field of our heart. We want to go into the field and immediately pull out every weed, but God says to let the two grow together until harvest time. For we cannot uproot the one without damaging the other.

There is a season of refining that God brings to burn off those things we've allowed to take root. It is the fire of His boundless love. The burning comes when a level of maturity is reached and the strength of the seed we have taken in is such that it can withstand the crucible of truth. What we have allowed to take root in our heart that is not of Him will be destroyed, and that which remains will be tested by the fire.

The goal of the Father is to build a royal priesthood that carries the name of Christ into the nations. A heart that has been purged of all fear about His faithfulness and mistrust of His goodness, is one that He considers worthy to receive ever increasing wisdom and insights from heaven.

QUIET REFLECTIONS _____

When you reflect on the fire of God, do you think about His grace and goodness? Or, do you fear it as judgment and condemnation? Psalms 51 reveals to us how David viewed the love of God. In his prayer seeking forgiveness, he notes that God desires truth in the inward parts of man's heart. (See verse 6.) When God brings His refiner's fire to you, will you open up to receive it, or turn from His burning gaze?

_____ **PRAYER TIME**

Heavenly Father, I thank You that You are a faithful God and that Your mercies are new every morning. Make me to know Your ways, O God. Cause me to walk in Your abiding truth. I cry out as David did and ask that You create in me a clean heart and that You renew a steadfast spirit in me. Thank You for Your unfailing love. I love You, Lord, and I bless what You are doing in my life. Amen.

My Personal Reflections

_____

_____

_____

_____

_____

_____

_____

_____

_____

_____

_____

_____

_____

_____

_____

_____

_____

My God Speaks

_____

_____

_____

_____

_____

_____

_____

_____

_____

_____

_____

_____

_____

_____

_____

_____

"When we find ourselves in seasons of spiritual famine it's easy to place our hope in people instead of God. However, misplaced hope can never birth newness of life or freedom. Misplaced hope blinds us to the goodness of a loving Father. "

DAY
6

MISPLACED HOPE

Then Elimelech, Naomi's husband, died; and she was left, and her two sons.

~(Ruth 1:3, NKJV)

Everything about this land of Moab was different to Naomi. The customs were different, the people acted differently, and they looked at life from a different point of view. Not to mention their religion was very different from what she knew and believed.

While the things she loved of her homeland were no longer surrounding her, and her extended family was far from her, she could at least let her hope rest in the nearness and familiarity of her husband and sons and she poured herself into caring for them. Before long she settled into her new life. Her husband was working hard to provide a good home for them and she trusted that he would get them through this season of separation.

What she didn't count on was the setback coming from Elimelech's faltering and failing hope-seed. Sadly, the continued pressures of living a life without hope, without any expectation for something better, quickly took its toll on Elimelech. When the seed of hope is allowed to die, the ultimate outcome is that life itself is strangled out.

Throughout her grieving process Naomi clung to the fact that her sons would be there to take care of her, and she would not be subject to the rejection and abandonment other widows of her day had to endure. She chose to put her trust in the kindness and care of her sons rather than in the goodness of her God.

When we find ourselves in seasons of spiritual famine it's easy to place our hope in people instead of God. However, misplaced hope can never birth newness of life or freedom. Misplaced hope blinds us to the goodness of a loving Father. We lose sight of who He is and move Him out of His rightful place as the head of our lives. We develop the belief that God has moved away from us, when in fact, it is we who have moved away from Him.

At the loss of her husband, Naomi could have made the decision to move the family back home to be nearer the extended family. They chose instead to stay in a land filled with broken dreams and false gods. They became so comfortable in a place of separation, they willingly stayed there.

QUIET REFLECTIONS _____

Experiencing separation is a common human emotion and can stem from any number of circumstances and challenges we face day to day. When you've experienced times of separation in the past, what did you do? What are the circumstances surrounding it? King David found himself in a season of separation from his family and friends. According to First Samuel 30:6, David encouraged himself in the Lord, and then sought out God's guidance. Hebrews 13:5 says that God will never leave us or forsake us. The Amplified Bible says He will never relax His hold on us. Be encouraged in His faithfulness today. While you may be feeling a sense of separation, He has never left you and He won't let go!

_____ **PRAYER TIME**

Father I thank You for Your promise to never let me go. As I come before You now I take courage in Your promise to always be with me. Forgive me Father for not trusting You as I should. Show me the areas where I have allowed my hope to rest in someone or something other than in You and Your goodness. I thank You for Your unfailing love for me and I bless what You are doing in my life. Amen.

My Personal Reflections

My God Speaks

_____

_____

_____

_____

_____

_____

_____

_____

_____

_____

_____

_____

_____

_____

_____

_____

_____

"Lost hope coupled with fear can cause us to join things together that God never intended to be joined together. God-ordained joinings have the power to bring new life. God would never join friendship with sickness."

DAY
7

LOST HOPE

Now they took wives of the women of Moab: the name of the one was Orpah, and the name of the other Ruth. And they dwelt there about ten years. Then both Mahlon and Chilion also died.

~(Ruth 1:4-5, NKJV)

Sometime after the death of their father, Mahlon and Chilion selected wives for themselves from the Moabites they were living among. The first son, Mahlon, whose name means "sickness," chose Ruth, or "friendship." Chilion, which means "wasting away," makes the selection of Orpah, whose name means "stiff-necked." Neither union had the power to produce children.

Naomi was not only willing to stay in Moab after Elimelech's death, but her sons were quite willing to assimilate into the culture by marrying into it. So deeply had the influence of the culture permeated their hearts that they were willing to align themselves at every level—socially, spiritually, mentally, and physically—to its beliefs and practices. Survival mode had slipped into complete acceptance mode and the mindsets and core values of the Moabite culture became their own.

Lost hope coupled with fear can cause us to join things together that God never intended to be joined together. God-ordained joinings have the power to bring new life. God would never join friendship with sickness. His plan for intimacy never joins us with lack, insufficiency, or infirmity of mind or soul.

These same relationships that had no power to produce new life also had no power to sustain existing life. After a decade of marriage, a decade of trying to produce something by self-effort, a decade of brokenness mingled with barrenness, both sons pass away leaving their wives as widows.

For ten years Ruth poured into a relationship with Mahlon that could not pour back into her. God did not allow a pregnancy to come from their union because it would have been birthed in hopelessness and would have kept the seed of hopelessness carrying forward in the family line.

Relationships that are not God-ordained were never designed to be your support system and when you stay connected to them, you cut off the power of hope in your life. They are life-draining and not life-giving or life-affirming. When you are cut off from the power of hope, you are cut off from the power that produces in you, and through you, the future you were designed to live.

QUIET REFLECTIONS _____

What types of relationships do you have in your life? Are they life-giving, affirming relationships? Or, do they drain you of strength and hope? Which relationships connect you to the power of hope in your life? Do you see places where you have moved out of survival mode and into acceptance mode—where you have accepted a way of believing that is not aligned to the truth of God's Word?

_____ **PRAYER TIME**

Father I thank You that as I linger before You now, You are showing me the influence and power of the relationships I have within my life and how each one affects me. Help me to distinguish those that have been ordained by You and those I need to let go. Connect me with the power of hope and help me to offer life-giving, life-affirming love to others. I thank You for Your unfailing love for me and I bless what You are doing in my life. Amen.

My Personal Reflections

_____
_____
_____
_____
_____
_____
_____
_____
_____
_____
_____
_____
_____
_____
_____
_____

My God Speaks

_____

_____

_____

_____

_____

_____

_____

_____

_____

_____

_____

_____

_____

_____

_____

_____

"While Naomi rehearsed her memories,

the breeze she remembered began stirring

again. It carried with it a whispered story

that began to tickle her ear with

the sound of fresh hope."

DAY
8

SURROUNDED BY BAD NEWS

---

*Then she arose with her daughters-in-law that she might
return from the country of Moab, for she had heard in the
country of Moab that the LORD had visited His people by
giving them bread.*

~(Ruth 1:6-7, NKJV)

Naomi was surrounded with nothing but bad news for
so long that she started believing God's hand had
turned against her. It took her awhile to realize what
she was really missing was the cradling touch and intimacy of
a loving Father's presence. It wasn't until the moment of her
greatest loss that she even recognized her need for something
more than what she had been living. When she was empty and
void in one area, she began feeling pain in other areas—the pain
from recognizing there is a missing piece to the puzzle of life.

Somewhere in her memory banks Naomi held a picture of the
experience of God's presence. It seemed like another lifetime

now, but there had been a time when she would whisper His sweet name and listened as He whispered a reply in her heart. She would slip away to a quiet place where it seemed she could hear the sound of His laughter in the wind, and feel His gentle touch as the breeze played across her face.

While Naomi rehearsed her memories, the breeze she remembered began stirring again. It carried with it a whispered story that began to tickle her ear with the sound of fresh hope.

Could it be true, she wondered? Was the famine over in Israel? The more she thought about what she was hearing the more her seed of hope began to vibrate until it reached such a point of churning she knew what she must do. She must return to the place where she felt Him last. She must return to the land of Judah.

Naomi made the decision to cast her *seed of hope* in the direction of the sound of hope she was hearing from home. The *word of hope* carried over the wind, down through the city streets and into Naomi's house. God sent the *sound of hope* right to Naomi's front door.

QUIET REFLECTIONS _____

Have you ever moved out in faith and then felt like God abandoned you? What did you do when you encountered opposition and struggle? Take a moment and reflect on the times when you allowed negative people or negative thoughts to affect your seed of hope. What can you do differently so it doesn't happen again? What does hope sound like to you? How will you respond to its sound?

_____ **PRAYER TIME**

Father, I thank You that You are revealing to me the areas where I've allowed negativity to affect my thinking. Cleanse me of the seeds of negativity that have taken root in my heart and plant again Your hope-seeds. I ask for a bountiful harvest of renewed hope to come into my life now. Cause my ears to hear the sound of hope and my mouth to speak words of hope. I thank You Father, for Your tender care and I bless what You are doing in my life. Amen.

My Personal Reflections

_____

_____

_____

_____

_____

_____

_____

_____

_____

_____

_____

_____

_____

_____

_____

_____

My God Speaks

_____

_____

_____

_____

_____

_____

_____

_____

_____

_____

_____

_____

_____

_____

_____

_____

_____

"When we listen we can hear a word behind us, reminding us of the goodness of the Lord. When you hear the sound, cast your hope in its direction. He will guide you back to the land of the living, into a place of connection with the Father..."

DAY
9

A WORD BEHIND YOU

***

And thine ears shall hear a word behind thee, saying, "This is the way, walk ye in it, when ye turn to the right hand, and when ye turn to the left."

~(Isaiah 30:21)

Life has a way of taking so many twists and turns that we can find ourselves backed into a corner facing a do-or-die moment: give up the dream and stay in a place of brokenness, or take the risk and make the move in the direction of hope's calling.

The decision to leave Moab would put a tremendous demand on the seed of hope within Naomi and her daughters-in-law. They had no way of knowing if the situation they were heading into was any better than the one they were leaving behind. They could be jumping in the river of fulfilled dreams, or into a sea of disaster.

God saw them exactly where they were, both physically and spiritually. He knew they were living in a place of doubt and discord emotionally that corresponded to the place of barrenness in their souls. He also knew it was time to do something about it, and so He sent a word.

When we listen we can hear a word behind us, reminding us of the goodness of the Lord. When you hear the sound, cast your hope in its direction. He will guide you back to the land of the living, into a place of connection with the Father, back to the house of bread—a place where you are feeding on His goodness and the awareness of His presence.

Jesus said these words to us in the book of Matthew: *"It is written, 'Man shall not live by bread alone, but by every word that proceeds from the mouth of God'"* (Matthew 4:4, NKJV).

We have to make the decision to follow the preceding word, or the word that was *spoken prior* to the circumstance we find ourselves in. There comes a point when we must choose to let go of what we have, what we know, and even what we want in order to move into what God has for us.

When Naomi looked back in the direction of her history, she discovered a word of provision that had been spoken and now was making its way straight to her. All she had to do was follow its leading.

God is always faithful to provide a fresh word to us. Continuing to follow His proceeding word will keep us moving forward into all He has for us. Don't get stuck in the last word given, keep listening for what He is saying right now.

Quiet Reflections _____

When you look back over your history, when were the times when you heard a word that offered you guidance? What action did you take when you heard it? As specifically as you can, describe what the Lord is speaking to you now in this moment. How will you respond?

_____ **Prayer Time**

Father, I thank You that You see me exactly where I am today and that You have a plan to set me in a large place of abundance and fulfillment. As I humble myself before You now I ask that You speak Your words of life and truth into my heart that I might follow You more closely. I thank You for the proceeding word. I love You and I bless what You are doing in my life. Amen.

My Personal Reflections

_____

_____

_____

_____

_____

_____

_____

_____

_____

_____

_____

_____

_____

_____

_____

_____

_____

My God Speaks

_____

_____

_____

_____

_____

_____

_____

_____

_____

_____

_____

_____

_____

_____

_____

_____

"Because conditional love was all she knew,

Naomi's sense of value came from her

ability to produce something others could

benefit from. She believed their loyalty was

not based in love, but instead in a desire to

gain from the relationship."

DAY
10

UNCONDITIONAL LOVE

Love suffers long and is kind; love does not envy; love does not parade itself, is not puffed up; does not behave rudely, does not seek its own, is not provoked, thinks no evil; does not rejoice in iniquity, but rejoices in the truth; bears all things, believes all things, hopes all things, endures all things. Love never fails.

~(1 Corinthians 13:4-8, NKJV)

Naomi and her daughters-in-law soon found themselves traveling through difficult country on a long fifty-mile journey from Moab to Naomi's hometown of Bethlehem. All along the way Naomi tried her best to get her traveling companions to turn around and go back to their homeland because she felt she had nothing of value left to offer. She hit them with a barrage of questions based on her own feelings of inadequacy.

A deep truth about Naomi's heart is revealed in the fact that she continually questions Ruth and Orpah about why they were going with her. The kind of love Naomi was used to receiving was not one of selflessness, but rather one based on conditions.

Because conditional love was all she knew, Naomi's sense of value came from her ability to produce something others could benefit from. She believed their loyalty was not based in love, but instead in a desire to gain from the relationship. Since Naomi believed her ability to produce was gone, she saw no reason for Ruth and Orpah to stick with her. (See Ruth 1:8-14.)

Conditional love is based in fear. It could be the fear of being rejected, or the fear of being hurt, or the fear of having the demands of others placed on us. Living in fear means we are not living in the full awareness of God's perfect love.

In contrast, God's love truly is unconditional. It is not based on what we do or say, or how we look. In fact, His love is not even based on our loving Him in return.

The Apostle John describes it this way: *"This is how God showed his love for us: God sent his only Son into the world so we might live through him. This is the kind of love we are talking about—not that we once upon a time loved God, but that he loved us and sent his Son as a sacrifice to clear away our sins and the damage they've done to our relationship with God"* (1 John 4:9-10, The Message).

God has never loved us with strings attached. The degree of His love for us never waivers, shifts, or changes in intensity. Nothing we do can cause Him to love us any more or any less. It is His ability to love us perfectly that casts out all fear and gives us the kind of hope we can use to build our future upon.

QUIET REFLECTIONS _____

How have you experienced conditional love in your life? Have you been on the giving or receiving side of it? When you think of the ways God shows His love to you, what comes to mind? Be specific. Take a few moments and read First John 4 and then write down the things God shows you as you reflect on His love.

_____ **PRAYER TIME**

Heavenly Father, I thank You that You continually show me unconditional love. You love me with no strings attached. Knowing that my love at times wavers, and yes even fails, You love me still. Teach me how to love unconditionally as You do. I want to be a living example of Your love in this life that I may bring glory to Your name. I love You, Lord, and I bless what You are doing in my life. Amen.

My Personal Reflections

_____

_____

_____

_____

_____

_____

_____

_____

_____

_____

_____

_____

_____

_____

_____

_____

_____

_____

My God Speaks

_____

_____

_____

_____

_____

_____

_____

_____

_____

_____

_____

_____

_____

_____

_____

_____

"Excess baggage from our past crams our hearts and clutters our minds with so many other things that we have no room left for the important ones. When our hands are filled with the baggage of our past we can't get a grip on the essentials needed to feed our dreams."

DAY
11

EXCESS BAGGAGE

Therefore I say to you, do not worry about your life, what you will eat or what you will drink; nor about your body, what you will put on. Is not life more than food and the body more than clothing?

~(Matthew 6:25-26, NKJV)

It would take Naomi and Ruth at least three days on the road walking the fifty miles from their home in Moab back to Bethlehem in Judah. The only possessions they had were the ones they could bundle together into a pack and carry with them. Most of the space in their packs would be taken up with provisions for the journey, so any other possessions they carried would by necessity be only those things that were most precious to them.

Just as they could bring no excess baggage with them into their future, God wants us to also walk lightly. Naomi and Ruth were being challenged to let go of old relationships, old beliefs, old habits, and anything else that would keep them bound to their past. The only thing they held tightly from their past life was each other. Bound together by the cords of love and common hope they traveled on toward their destination.

Excess baggage only serves one purpose—to weigh us down. Have you ever overpacked for vacation, cramming your suitcases so full that you pull your back out trying to haul it all through the airport? The same is true in the spiritual sense as well. When we carry excess baggage we pull ourselves out of alignment with God and His purposes.

Excess baggage from our past crams our hearts and clutters our minds with so many other things that we have no room left for the important ones. When our hands are filled with the baggage of our past we can't get a grip on the essentials needed to feed our dreams.

The vessels we used to hold the bits and pieces of our past life cannot serve us in our future because they are shaped by our past experiences. New wine put into an old wine skin will break down the container and spoil the new wine. New experiences, like new wine, must have a new vessel—one without set limitations from the previous content.

QUIET REFLECTIONS _____

Gideon gathered no less than 30,000 men to go to war with him. He believed he had what he needed for the job at hand. Except God had a different idea, and when He finished paring down the excess, Gideon was left with 300 men. (See Judges 6:1-7:5). Sometimes what we think we need to carry with us for the battles and victories that lie ahead is not what we need at all. What are you carrying in this season that God is asking you to lay down? Knowing that letting go of one thing allows you to get a grip on something else, what is it that you are wanting to reach for?

_____ **PRAYER TIME**

Father, I thank You for Your faithful and loving care. I ask You to show me the things I need to let go of in this season. Uncover and separate me from the beliefs and mindsets that have held me back and keep me locked in regret and unfruitfulness. Create in me a clean, new vessel that You can deposit Your truth into. I thank You for Your tender mercies and I bless what You are doing in my life. Amen.

My Personal Reflections

_____

_____

_____

_____

_____

_____

_____

_____

_____

_____

_____

_____

_____

_____

_____

_____

My God Speaks

_____

_____

_____

_____

_____

_____

_____

_____

_____

_____

_____

_____

_____

_____

_____

_____

_____

_____

"The question of intention is one God usually has to force on us because it's such a difficult one to answer. The difficulty lies in the fact that we have to get gut-level honest with ourselves about what it is we really are hoping for."

DAY
12

THE QUESTION OF INTENTION

---

*But Naomi said, "Turn back, my daughters; why will you go
with me? Are there still sons in my womb, that they may be
your husbands? Turn back, my daughters, go—for I am too
old to have a husband. If I should say I have hope, if I should
have a husband tonight and should also bear sons, would
you wait for them till they were grown? Would you restrain
yourselves from having husbands? No, my daughters; for
it grieves me very much for your sakes that the hand of the
LORD has gone out against me!*

~(Ruth 1:11-13, NKJV)

Naomi continued questioning Ruth and Orpah as they
traveled along. Somewhere along their journey, in
between where they were and where they were going,
the question of intention came up.

Naomi had already settled her decision to go back home to
Bethlehem, but the intention of her two traveling companions

was not as clear. Naomi takes up her questions again to her daughters-in-law, "Why are you following me? Do I yet have sons in my womb that they may be your husbands?" The real question that needed to be answered was, "What is it that you hope to find when you arrive?"

Her question serves to reveal the real desires of her two followers. In this moment of processing, one woman discovers her heart is set on her future, and one discovers she never really let go of her past. One is hoping to find her destiny, while the other realizes her hopes are still tied to her history and the place she came from.

The question of intention is one God usually has to force on us because it's such a difficult one to answer. The difficulty lies in the fact that we have to get gut-level honest with ourselves about what it is we really are hoping for.

Orpah and Ruth had to decide what they wanted before they could move any further into their journey. Until we know what "it" is that we are hoping for, we won't be able to recognize "it" when we finally touch it. Answering the question of intention requires that you see yourself in your future. By catching a glimpse of yourself there, it will give you something to grab hold of to pull yourself forward.

Orpah was caught up in the whirlwind of questions in her own mind. Perhaps you've asked the same questions. How will it happen? Will I be able to? Am I strong enough to let go of what I have to grab hold of what I want?

The point Orpah missed, (and we do, too) was that the answer to these questions won't come until you answer the bigger question: "What do I want?"

Ruth's intention was to make a better life for herself and for her mother-in-law, Naomi. She set all the other questions swirling around in her heart to the side and kept her focus set. Once she settled the question of intention in her heart, she stuck to it and kept her feet moving in the direction of her vision.

The question of intention requires focused attention. The place Orpah turns away from the possibility of a better life, is the same place Ruth makes a different decision. The grip Orpah had on her past was stronger than the pull of her future. In contrast, Ruth says, "Don't force me to leave you." Regardless of what lay ahead, Ruth made the decision to stick it out. Wherever Naomi's journey took her, Ruth was determined to be by her side.

QUIET REFLECTIONS _____

What is it you hope to find in your future? Do you know the desire of your heart? What questions are coming to the surface now as you focus on your desire? What fears are coming up? By giving the Father permission to search your heart and bring to light what is laying in the hidden corners, He will help you discover what "it" is that you really desire. And then He'll guide you every step of the way until you lay hold of it.

_____ PRAYER TIME

Father, I give You permission to search me as You help me discover the desires of my heart. I ask that You grant me wisdom and understanding on this journey of discovery. I release all my unanswered questions to You, as well as my need to have them all answered. Help me to make the decision as Ruth did, to move into my future with determination and intention. I love You, Lord, and I bless what You are doing in my life. Amen.

YOUR FOOD FOR THOUGHT MOMENT

Intention is the key to progress. Without it, you would never take one step forward! God was intentional when He set about creating a world filled with everything man could possibly need, then He intentionally set man down in his established place.

For which of you, **intending to build** *a tower, does not sit down first and count the cost, whether he has enough to finish it—lest, after he has laid the foundation, and is not able to finish, all who see it begin to mock him, saying, 'This man began to build and was not able to finish.'* (Luke 14:28-30, NKJV, *emphasis added*).

This passage relates a simple but profound truth as it relates to being intentional. To build anything—a home, a business, or a new life—you must be intentional. Our desire becomes our intention.

Proverbs says, "Keep vigilant watch over your heart; that's where life starts." (Proverbs 4:23, The Message Bible). In other words, life begins at the point of your intention.

Intentional people become influencers. Intentional people have decision making power. Intentional people are willing to count the cost to make a difference. It's time to be intentional!

My Personal Reflections

_____

_____

_____

_____

_____

_____

_____

_____

_____

_____

_____

_____

_____

_____

_____

_____

My God Speaks

"When we begin to devalue ourselves our speech changes. And when our speech changes, others around us begin seeing us differently and in turn, change how they value us."

DAY
13

FRIENDSHIP AND BITTERNESS

Then they lifted up their voices and wept again; and Orpah kissed her mother-in-law, but Ruth clung to her. And she said, "Look, your sister-in-law has gone back to her people and to her gods; return after your sister-in-law." But Ruth said: "Entreat me not to leave you, or to turn back from following after you; for wherever you go, I will go; and wherever you lodge, I will lodge; your people shall be my people, and your God, my God. Where you die, I will die, and there will I be buried. The LORD do so to me, and more also, if anything but death parts you and me." When she saw that she was determined to go with her, she stopped speaking to her.

~(Ruth 1:14-18, NKJV)

With the death of their husbands, Naomi and Ruth lost their identity within the culture of their day. Widows were not held in great regard; in fact it was common for them to be neglected by society. When we lose our identity we lose our destiny; when we lose our destiny we lose our sense of value. When we begin to devalue ourselves our speech changes. And when our speech changes, others around us begin seeing us differently and in turn, change how they value us.

Naomi's sense of value hit such a low it pushed her to change how she called herself and how she expected others to see her. When we peer into their arrival in Bethlehem, we discover how she is interpreting her own life events. She tells the women of the city to start calling her Mara, or "bitter."

In contrast, Ruth's name in Hebrew means "friendship." Here is the heart of Ruth's life-changing decision—friendship made the choice to align herself with a bitter woman. It was the power of intention that forged an unbreakable bond between friendship and bitterness. What was it that Ruth saw in Naomi that caused her to stay connected to her? No one chooses to connect to a bitter person, so there must have been something that Ruth knew or saw about Naomi's character before the circumstances of life had formed her into the bitter woman she was now.

Ruth decided to step outside of herself and the pain she was feeling, to connect to someone whose pain was even greater than her own. Ruth had lost her husband, but Naomi had lost her husband and both her sons. Ruth's decision became a life-changing event for both of them that encompassed every aspect of their daily lives. She held fast to Naomi, choosing an arduous journey into the unfamiliar territory of self-discovery. In the process, the label of Ruth the Moabite fell away and she became known as Ruth—a friend, part of the bloodline of the Messiah. And she stayed connected with Naomi until both of them could walk out of their pain and into the new life God had for them.

QUIET REFLECTIONS _____

Who are the top five people in your life you are connected to? How are you connected? What were the circumstances that brought you together? What are the reasons you stay connected? Are there relationships where you need to connect on a deeper level? How about relationships you need to disconnect from?

_____ PRAYER TIME

Jesus, I thank You for being my Savior and Lord. I thank You for providing a way for me to reconnect with my heavenly Father, and I thank You for helping me to see more clearly the relationships in my life and how they affect my seed of hope. I pray for divine connections and preordained relationships. I love You, Lord, and I bless what You are doing in my life. Amen.

My Personal Reflections

My God Speaks

_____

_____

_____

_____

_____

_____

_____

_____

_____

_____

_____

_____

_____

_____

_____

_____

_____

"The once joy-filled Naomi was now buried deep under all the heartbreak. Bitterness has a way of working down into the heart once it finds a lodging place in the mind. Its power is so great that everything we say and do becomes tainted with the taste of bitterness."

DAY
14

A HEART OF BITTERNESS

Now the two of them went until they came to Bethlehem. And it happened, when they had come to Bethlehem, that all the city was excited because of them; and the women said, "Is this Naomi?" But she said to them, "Do not call me Naomi; call me Mara, for the Almighty has dealt very bitterly with me. I went out full, and the LORD has brought me home again empty. Why do you call me Naomi, since the LORD has testified against me, and the Almighty has afflicted me?"

~(Ruth 1:19-21, NKJV)

To say the least, Naomi and Ruth were exhausted when they finally arrived. Naomi looked so different from when she left ten years earlier that her friends had trouble recognizing her when she arrived back in Bethlehem. Her body was frail, and she looked haggard and beaten down by life. The beauty that had turned heads in her youth had fled from her. Instead, there were deep lines of sorrow etched into her face. Her step was heavy, her back bent. But she followed the call of hope and came back home anyway.

As they made their way through the city gates, Naomi caught the sounds of whispered speech around her. It seems she and her traveling companion were attracting a lot of attention. The snatches of conversation all buzzed around the same question, "Is that Naomi?"

Their return caused such a stir that the entire city took notice. As they made their way along, the women of Bethlehem questioned Naomi about her ten-year absence. She summed up a decade of her life with the words, "Call me bitter."

She couldn't get past the bitterness left in her heart. She had spent the last three days and fifty miles rehearsing all the reasons why she was bitter and why she felt God had abandoned her. How could she explain her lost family and lost identity in a few simple sentences? All the events of her life had amassed together into a block of pain resting deep down in the core of her being. So deep was the pain that she began to identify herself by her bitter experiences. She wanted others to identify with her in her pain also, so she asked to be called Mara or "bitter," instead of Naomi or "pleasant."

The once joy-filled Naomi was now buried deep under all the heartbreak. Bitterness has a way of working down into the heart once it finds a lodging place in the mind. Its power is so great that everything we say and do becomes tainted with the taste of bitterness.

Naomi may have been feeling bitter about her life, her situation, and even bitter toward her God. But God wasn't bitter toward Naomi. In fact, He wasn't quite finished with her. He had a job for her to do, so He set about to turn her captivity and complete the restoration of hope in her life. His plan only began with sending out the sound of hope to lead her back home to Bethlehem. Once she was there He set her up for a cascade effect of good things that wiped away every ounce of bitterness from her soul.

Quiet Reflections _____

Proverbs 14:10 says, "The heart knows its own bitterness, and a stranger does not share its joy." The heart keeps a record of the anguish we feel, the sorrows we face, and the pain we endure. However, with God's help, we don't have to let that record rule our lives. We can make the choice to let go of the pain in favor of the joy and peace He offers. Does your heart carry any bitterness?

_____ **Prayer Time**

Father, I thank You for Your grace and truth and the power of Your active love in my life. I ask that You show me the events and circumstances where I have allowed a root of bitterness to form in my heart. I bring myself into agreement with Your truth and ask that You uproot whatever is in my heart that is not of You. I love You, and I bless what You are doing in my life. Amen.

My Personal Reflections

_____

_____

_____

_____

_____

_____

_____

_____

_____

_____

_____

_____

_____

_____

_____

My God Speaks

_____

_____

_____

_____

_____

_____

_____

_____

_____

_____

_____

_____

_____

_____

_____

_____

"God knew Naomi carried the potential to facilitate connections in the natural realm that would bring about powerful connections in the spiritual realm. All the while she felt fulfilled, God knew she hadn't even begun to touch her real purpose."

DAY
15

FINDING FULFILLMENT

I went out full, and the LORD has brought me home again empty. Why do you call me Naomi, since the LORD has testified against me, and the Almighty has afflicted me?

~(Ruth 1:21, NKJV)

When Naomi left Bethlehem ten years earlier she considered herself to be living at her fullest potential, her zenith, her apex. She was married to a good husband who was well known and considered to be a leader in the community; she had two beautiful boys whom she loved dearly; and, unlike others who were forced to sell off their property, they would have land and a home to return to one day when they were ready. In her eyes, she had obtained the fullness of her destiny in being a wife and a mother. God, however, saw things a little differently.

By the time she returns to Bethlehem the bitterness of her soul has changed her way of expressing herself, her posture, and her walk—in essence, her way of being.

Her speech was laced with bitterness; every expression coming from her was now tainted with the bitter taste of a lingering sorrow. Her posture shifted as well. She no longer positioned herself in expectancy to receive a blessing from God. Her hands were not raised in joyful return, nor her head lifted in the hope of favor. She no longer walked in faith that God was well able and that He had her best interest in mind.

She believed God had stripped her of everything she found fulfilling. She saw herself as coming back empty. However, God saw her as coming back full of potential. What she counted as loss, God counted as a stripping away of hindrances that would prevent her from reaching what He considered her fullness. It is when we are emptied of those things we consider our fullness that God can reveal our purpose.

God knew Naomi carried the potential to facilitate connections in the natural realm that would bring about powerful connections in the spiritual realm. All the while she felt fulfilled, God knew she hadn't even begun to touch her real purpose. Naomi was destined to connect the principal of truth represented by Boaz, to the affections of truth represented by Ruth. Without her ability to make the connection, a future king would never be born.

QUIET REFLECTIONS _____

What are the things in your life that bring you fulfillment? Has God ever removed any from your life and if so, how did you respond? With anger, resentment or bitterness? Or did you see it as a blessing to bring you into the destiny He has for you?

_____ **PRAYER TIME**

Father, I thank You. You are my peace and the hope of my strength. I ask that You reveal to me the things I am finding fulfillment in that have nothing to do with my destiny. Cause me to desire the things You have for me and help me to find my fulfillment in You. I love You and I bless what You are doing in my life. Amen.

My Personal Reflections

My God Speaks

_____

_____

_____

_____

_____

_____

_____

_____

_____

_____

_____

_____

_____

_____

_____

"It is faith that waters the seed

of hope. Faith, hope, and love is a

three-strand cord that cannot

easily be broken..."

DAY
16

LOOKING FOR FAVOR

―――――――― ⟨≈≈≈⟩ ――――――――

So Ruth the Moabitess said to Naomi, "Please let me go to the field, and glean heads of grain after him in whose sight I may find favor." And she said to her, "Go, my daughter." Then she left, and went and gleaned in the field after the reapers. And she happened to come to the part of the field belonging to Boaz, who was of the family of Elimelech.

~(Ruth 2:2-3, NKJV)

Ruth initially asks for permission to glean because she is living in a state known as survival mode. Part of her heart expects to find favor, while part expects to find just enough to live on. God however, not only grants her enough for the present but an abundance for the future. It begins with the favor she finds with the head servant, the one in charge of all the reapers. He not only allows her to glean after the reapers, but also allows her to rest in the shed where only the harvesters were allowed to take a break and rest.

Gleaning was a system set up by God in the Old Testament to provide for the widows, the fatherless, and those living temporally in the land of Israel. However, it was not guaranteed that one would be allowed to glean. The decision rested with the landowner to either grant favor or to withhold it.

Ruth set out in faith that she would find favor that very day! It is faith that waters the seed of hope. Faith, hope, and love is a three-strand cord that cannot easily be broken. The fear that had been her constant companion was now replaced with faith—a steady belief that things were going to work out in her favor.

The expectation of favor comes from the power of an activated seed of hope. She goes out expecting to find enough grain from her gleaning to sustain them through the coming months and into the next harvest season. Believing she would encounter favor caused her to put feet to her faith by taking the next logical step. When God sees faith on the move He is obligated to honor it. She "happens upon" the field of Boaz and falls right into the favor she was looking for all along. Although, the level of favor she was expecting turned out to be nothing compared to the level she received!

An activated seed of hope requires action to sustain it and feed it for continued growth. Ruth took the action of going into the field, setting her hands to work finding the necessary food they needed to live. She goes out in humbleness of heart with the request, "May

I follow after the harvesters?" Casting her hope out in front of her, it draws her (by what seems to be chance) into the field of Boaz—the very man God intended her to meet all along.

QUIET REFLECTIONS _____

The word gleaning means to extract from various sources. As believers, our sources can be the Word, inspirational writings, and fellowship with other believers. What are the fields where you are gleaning? Ruth went out to glean with the expectation of finding favorable results that would support her in the current season and guide her into the future. Are the sources you are gleaning from viable to sustain you in the current season? Will they be sufficient to sustain you in your future?

_____ PRAYER TIME

Thank You, Father for Your good care and tender mercies. I thank You that You have provided ways to sustain and support the seed of hope You have given me. I pray that You would guide me into pathways of Your favor and grant me the blessing of growing in the knowledge of You and Your grace. I love You, and I bless what You are doing in my life. Amen.

My Personal Reflections

_____

_____

_____

_____

_____

_____

_____

_____

_____

_____

_____

_____

_____

_____

_____

_____

My God Speaks

_____

_____

_____

_____

_____

_____

_____

_____

_____

_____

_____

_____

_____

_____

_____

_____

_____

_____

"Every seed of hope needs the fellowship of like-minded seed holders. It is this partnership of faith where like-minded people come together to build a dream that nurtures the seed of hope until it blossoms into the full tree of life encoded within its design."

DAY
17

ADVICE FROM A WISE COUNSELOR

So the servant who was in charge of the reapers answered and said, "It is the young Moabite woman who came back with Naomi from the country of Moab. And she said, 'Please let me glean and gather after the reapers among the sheaves.' So she came and has continued from morning until now, though she rested a little in the house." Then Boaz said to Ruth, "You will listen, my daughter, will you not? Do not go to glean in another field, nor go from here, but stay close by my young women. Let your eyes be on the field which they reap, and go after them. Have I not commanded the young men not to touch you? And when you are thirsty, go to the vessels and drink from what the young men have drawn."

~(Ruth 2:6-9, NKJV)

It didn't take Boaz long to realize there was something different about Ruth. He questions his head servant about her and the servant replies, "This is the Moabite woman that came back with Naomi." Boaz then turns to Ruth and gives her some poignant instruction.

First he tells her to stay in the same field and continue to follow after his reapers. If Ruth had moved to another field, her seed of hope would have been cut off from its source just as it was beginning to take root. Hope can't grow when it is continually uprooted and transplanted into other soil.

Once a seed is sown, the ground begins to adapt to the needs of the seed. The ground pulls from its rich resources to provide every nutrient needed to sustain the seed for continued growth. Everything the seed needs in its season of putting down roots and everything it will need in its future season of bringing forth fruit, is provided through the adaptability of the soil. Any seed pulled from its environment will lose its source of nourishment and thereby, lose its power to become what it was designed to be.

Boaz wanted Ruth to stay in the same field doing exactly what those around her were doing. She was not to wander off and begin to do her own thing in another corner of the field. Every seed of hope needs the fellowship of like-minded seed holders. It is this partnership of faith where like-minded people come together to build a dream that nurtures the seed of hope until it blossoms into the full tree of life encoded within its design.

Secondly, he tells her to keep her eyes on the field where they are harvesting. She was to stay attentive to the bigger picture of the greater field itself, not just the small area where she was working. When the harvesters moved on to another section of the field she was to follow after them.

Once hope begins to grow it cannot be contained in a small place. Hope needs room to branch out, to break forth into everything it was designed to be, and it needs plenty of space to do it. A tree is not meant to remain a sapling all its life. Contained within the design of the seed is the image of the towering oak. The oak within the seed must have enough space not only for its roots to expand, but also its branches.

Lastly, he tells her to drink from what the servants have drawn. He makes it clear to her that everything she needs to sustain her seed of hope in the season of its turning and becoming, will be there provided for her at the moment she needs it. God always makes provision for every need of the hope-seeds He gives.

QUIET REFLECTIONS _____

Have you provided a secure place for your hope-seed to be nurtured? Are you settled into the soil of a community of like-minded believers? What are the nutrients you are drawing from the soil in your field? Are you continually experiencing growth and expansion?

_____ **PRAYER TIME**

Thank You, Father, for the hope-seed You have placed in my heart. And I thank You for providing for its nurture and growth through Your Word and the guidance of Your Holy Spirit. I ask for Your continued blessing so my hope-seed can grow into the full tree of faith, love, and hope it is designed to become. I love You, Lord, and I bless what You are doing in my life. Amen.

My Personal Reflections

_____

_____

_____

_____

_____

_____

_____

_____

_____

_____

_____

_____

_____

_____

_____

My God Speaks

_____

_____

_____

_____

_____

_____

_____

_____

_____

_____

_____

_____

_____

_____

"There are times when it is easy to feel distant from God and His plan for our lives but we are not considered 'foreigners' by Him. In fact, He calls us bone of His bone and flesh of His flesh."

DAY
18

WHY ME?

So she fell on her face, bowed down to the ground, and said to him, "Why have I found favor in your eyes, that you should take notice of me, since I am a foreigner?" And Boaz answered and said to her, "It has been fully reported to me, all that you have done for your mother-in-law since the death of your husband, and how you have left your father and your mother and the land of your birth, and have come to a people whom you did not know before. The LORD repay your work, and a full reward be given you by the LORD God of Israel, under whose wings you have come for refuge." Then she said, "Let me find favor in your sight, my lord; for you have comforted me, and have spoken kindly to your maidservant, though I am not like one of your maidservants."

~(Ruth 2:10-13, NKJV)

Ruth was so overwhelmed by the generosity of Boaz and the favor he gave her, that she falls down prostrate at his feet and asks the question, "Why would you even take notice of me seeing that I am a foreigner?"

Her "why me" question is born out of her deep sense of disqualification. As a Moabite, Ruth came from a race of people who were apathetic, lacking in motivation, and indifferent to what the future held. She recognized that she was not part of the heritage of the children of Israel and really had no right to expect all the favor she was receiving from Boaz.

Boaz lets Ruth know that everything she thought disqualified her was wiped away by an act of selfless love when she surrendered her plans and her will to the plans and will of Naomi, no matter what it ultimately cost her. Like Jesus in the Garden of Gethsemane, this was Ruth's "Not my will, but thine be done" moment. It is a crossroad we all come to at some point in our journey; whose will are we going to obey? Our own, or our heavenly Father's?

There are times when it is easy to feel distant from God and His plan for our lives but we are not considered 'foreigners' by Him. In fact, He calls us bone of His bone and flesh of His flesh. In our case, the act of love is that of the Father shown to us by giving His Son to die for our sins. We have been made one with Him by His sacrifice on the cross.

Ruth felt disqualified by her past to receive even a handful of blessing left for her in her season of searching. The idea of blessing was "foreign" to her heart and to her way of thinking. Her heart and her head were telling her, "it's not possible for a woman with my background to have this much favor." And yet she was seeing and touching a realm she never dreamed possible. A realm where God's provision flows abundantly, a realm where Shalom rules—nothing missing, nothing broken.

After receiving the handfuls of blessing, Boaz then speaks a blessing of the double portion over her. He puts a demand on heaven for a continued blessing to be poured out over her work, and for a full recompense of all she lost in her previous season. He made it clear to a woman who considered herself disqualified that God is no respecter of persons, and she was now living under the smile of His favor.

QUIET REFLECTIONS _____

What are the moments in your life where you have felt disqualified to receive blessing or promotion? What were the "handfuls of blessing" God dropped in your path to guide you into a new way of believing? Ruth's blessing came through the people around her. Who are the people in your life that God is using right now to release blessing to you?

_____ **PRAYER TIME**

Heavenly Father, I thank You for the people You have placed in my life that have left a deposit of faith and blessing for me to feed upon. I thank You that I am not disqualified by my past to receive Your favor and blessing; and I thank You that You are moving me into a new season of a fresh awareness of Your goodness. I love You, Lord, and I bless what You are doing in my life. Amen.

My Personal Reflections

_____

_____

_____

_____

_____

_____

_____

_____

_____

_____

_____

_____

_____

_____

_____

_____

_____

My God Speaks

_____

_____

_____

_____

_____

_____

_____

_____

_____

_____

_____

_____

_____

_____

_____

_____

_____

_____

_____

"The blessings God bestows in our lives are not for us. That thought may seem counterintuitive, especially when we have gone through seasons of famine prior to the blessing. The truth is, the blessings we receive are for those around us to feed on."

DAY
19

FEEDING ON OVERFLOW

---

*So she gleaned in the field until evening, and beat out what
she had gleaned, and it was about an ephah of barley. Then
she took it up and went into the city, and her mother-in-law
saw what she had gleaned. So she brought out and gave to
her what she had kept back after she had been satisfied.*

~(Ruth 2:17-18, NKJV)

Ruth comes home that evening and tells Naomi about her
day and the favor she found from the owner of the field.
Then she pulls from her apron the leftovers from her
lunch and Naomi feeds on the overflow of Ruth's favor.

On her first day in the field she gleaned about a bushel of grain.
It was enough grain to last herself and her mother-in-law for the
next six days. Six is the number of man, it represents the day that
God created man. It is the number that marks man's striving or
self-effort.

The six days of grain Ruth gathers marks the beginning of her season of trusting God for her daily provision. She has already made the declaration that the God of Israel will be her God and now she begins to "work it out" by going into the field every day of the harvest season. She is expecting to gather enough in this season of work to carry them through the dry season, or the next season of lack, that is lurking just around the corner. The gods of her past were never gods of provision so she has no frame of reference to teach her about this God of Israel. She is just beginning to learn who He is. She has yet to discover that one of His names is Jehovah Jireh, the God of provision.

As she begins sharing her day's adventures, Naomi tells her to abide by the advice of Boaz and stay close to the other women in the field. And then she lets her know that Boaz is not just the owner of the field but also a close relative, close enough to redeem Ruth and break the cycle of poverty and self-preservation they were living in.

Ruth keeps going back day after day all the way through barley season and then through the wheat harvest. Each time she put feet to her faith, she met with favor. Every day for six months straight she brought home more than enough food for herself and Naomi.

The blessings God bestows in our lives are not for us. That thought may seem counterintuitive, especially when we have gone through seasons of famine prior to the blessing. The truth is, the blessings we receive are for those around us to feed on.

When we pass through dry seasons were it seems lack is our portion, we learn with greater awareness the goodness of the Father. Even though we may not be completely on the other side, we can still offer a guiding hand to someone behind us. God has a way of connecting us to people who need what we carry, even if we think it's just a meager handful. To those around us, our overflow of favor is a life-giving stream.

QUIET REFLECTIONS _____

God called Moses at a time when the Israelites had been living in Egypt nearly 400 years. When it came time for them to leave, God made supernatural provision for them by plundering their captors of the nation's wealth. They walked out one step at a time, carrying the overflow of blessing with them. How has God allowed you to use your overflow of blessing in the lives of those around you?

_____ **PRAYER TIME**

Heavenly Father, I thank You that You are my All Sufficient One. In You I find all my provision and I suffer no lack because You are the God of More Than Enough! You are a loving Father, always mindful of all my daily needs. And You cause Your goodness to overflow in my life by daily loading me up with Your benefits. You are a good, good Father! I love You, Lord, and I bless what You are doing in my life. Amen.

My Personal Reflections

My God Speaks

_____

_____

_____

_____

_____

_____

_____

_____

_____

_____

_____

_____

_____

_____

_____

_____

_____

"A glimpse into the future can only be seen accurately through eyes filled with hope. Without hope as our guide, our vision becomes clouded with fear and self-doubt."

DAY
20

WHERE WILL FAVOR TAKE YOU?

Then Naomi her mother-in-law said to her, "My daughter, shall I not seek security for you, that it may be well with you?

~(Ruth 3:1-2, NKJV)

When the end of harvest season finally arrives, Naomi gives instruction to Ruth once again. But first she asks her another question designed to uncover the desire of Ruth's heart. "Shall I not seek rest for you?" Or in today's vernacular, "Shall I not try to find a home for you?"

Once again the intention of Ruth's heart had to surface. Where did she want this favor she was living under to take her? Where would she cast her seed of hope next? Naomi was asking her to take a good look at her life and see into her future what wanted to emerge. What is out there just waiting for you to speak up?

A glimpse into the future can only be seen accurately through eyes filled with hope. Without hope as our guide, our vision becomes clouded with fear and self-doubt. The initial vibration and the subsequent planting of your seed of hope are only the beginning. How you let the seed grow determines the fruit you will bear.

Naomi's question also served to remind Ruth that the season of self-provision was over and she was now in the season of God-appointed provision.

It seems like a good opportunity for her to speak up and say exactly who she expects to become and what her future holds. She could have said something like, I want to have a nice home, have a loving family, have plenty of money—the list could go on! Instead, she simply says, "I will do whatever you tell me to do." Ruth's response determines her course for the rest of her life. So she cleans herself up, puts on her best dress, dabs on a little perfume, and heads out to the party Boaz was throwing at the threshing floor. After all the others leave the party, Boaz lies down by the threshed grain and falls asleep. This was a common practice so the owner could keep watch over his freshly harvested crop. However, sometime in the night he awakens, startled to find a woman lying at his feet.

Let's take a brief step back and look again at Naomi's advice. She told Ruth to lie down at Boaz's feet after he was asleep, then to take a corner of his blanket from his feet and cover herself with it. In those days it was customary for servants to sleep in the same tent or chamber as their master. If they wanted to be covered, custom also allowed for the servant to use the extremity of their master's covering over themselves. When Ruth made use of the blanket of Boaz she was giving him a subtle reminder that he was a close kinsman with the power to redeem her, or in other words, the power to become a covering for her.

The first thing Ruth's activated hope-seed attracted to her was provision for her daily needs. Secondly, it attracted her kinsman-redeemer, someone with the power to change the course of her future. She never dreamed that her hope-filled decision to follow Naomi out of Moab would bring her to such a level of protection and grace. Little did she know her hope-seed still held a bountiful, fruitful crop just ahead of her!

QUIET REFLECTIONS

Ruth's vision in Moab was cloudy, with her future appearing as a shadowy substance of possibility, but she kept pushing forward, even if it seemed only a small step at a time, into her future. Each step forward helped to anchor her hope-seed a little deeper in the soil of faith and love. In her own way, she followed Habakkuk's advice to "write the vision and make it plain."

Are you writing the vision? Do you have a dream board? If so, what are the things you have on it? If you don't have a dream board, consider making one. It will help to more clearly define your dream. Where do you want your hope-seed to take you next? Be specific.

PRAYER TIME

Father, I thank You for the way You provide for my daily needs. I call myself blessed of the Lord, for You are a good Father. You said in Your Word, "I know what I'm doing. I have it all planned out—plans to take care of you, not abandon you, plans to give you the future you hope for" (Jeremiah 29:11, The Message Bible). Because of this promise Father, I lay my hopes and plans before You now and ask You to direct my steps according to Your plans. I give You permission to adjust my thoughts, ideas, and strategies so that I may walk into the future You have planned for me. I love You, Lord, and I bless what You are doing in my life. Amen.

YOUR FOOD FOR THOUGHT MOMENT

It was favor that took Joseph into Pharaoh's court. But first it took him into a pit and a prison. While pits and prisons don't feel like places of favor, they were necessary components to experience the palace.

Psalms 5:12 says, "For You, O LORD, will bless the righteous; with favor You will surround him as with a shield" (NKJV). Favor is the armor God puts on His children. It is the shield we carry into battle.

The position God was moving Joseph into would require him to have great favor among the entire Egyptian government, as well as the general populace of the nation and the surrounding nations. People had to believe Joseph was the man with the answers. Before that could happen, the awareness of God's favor had to build within Joseph, creating a shield around his heart and mind against the days of lack and testing that were just around the corner.

God's favor begins for you long before you make it to your "palace." By the time Joseph stepped into the position of favor God had ordained was his, he was fully prepared for it because of the shield of favor surrounding him. The same is true of you. God's favor is surrounding you right now, in your present moment, and it will carry you to the place He has prepared for you.

My Personal Reflections

My God Speaks

_____

_____

_____

_____

_____

_____

_____

_____

_____

_____

_____

_____

_____

_____

_____

"We can only know ourselves by how others react or respond to us. Ruth recognized that her service was part of who she was and that she was most alive when she was serving others."

DAY
21

WHO ARE YOU—REALLY?

Now it happened at midnight that the man was startled, and turned himself; and there, a woman was lying at his feet. And he said, "Who are you?" So she answered, "I am Ruth, your maidservant. Take your maidservant under your wing, for you are a close relative."

~ (Ruth 3:8-9, NKJV)

A quest often begins with a question. This time the question was coming from the man who could change everything around for Ruth. But first, before she could take another step forward into her destiny, she needed to identify herself.

His simple question "Who are you?" once again invited Ruth to give expression to what was in her heart. "I am Ruth, and I'm your maidservant," she responds.

Knowing who we are involves embracing the scars of our past as part of our necessary journey to fulfilling our destiny. Scars are evidence of choices made. Will we choose to avoid the pain and remain where we are comfortable, or take the risk of discovering ourselves and reach for our future?

Ruth's seed of hope had a few scars etched into it—scars caused by the pain of losing her husband and her status in society; scars from moving to a place completely unfamiliar to her; and more scars from the responsibility of providing food and shelter for herself and Naomi. But she didn't let her scars define how her hope-seed would grow. In fact, she was grateful for each one, for without them she would never have reached Bethlehem where Boaz was waiting.

We can only know ourselves by how others react or respond to us. Ruth recognized that her service was part of who she was and that she was most alive when she was serving others. She had a better understanding of who she was because she was willing to see herself through the eyes of those God had set in her life.

Because of their deeply intertwined relationship, Naomi saw Ruth as she truly was, without the layers of her native country, Moab, on her. What she saw was a woman who walked in humility and wisdom. She saw Ruth was destined for a place of influence by how she conducted herself in the tough times. Based on the integrity of Ruth's heart, Naomi set out to connect Ruth to a prominent businessman.

She was careful to select someone known for his character and integrity, as well as his wisdom.

Through the eyes of Boaz, Ruth better understood the characteristics of her personality. She saw herself as a caring, concerned woman, one that was willing to serve. Boaz explained that the whole city recognized her as a women of excellence because of her treatment of Naomi.

Discovering the qualities that frame our character and personality is the result of interacting with others. Relationship is the tool God uses to bring out our best; and though we don't want to admit it, to uncover our worst.

Because of Ruth's interactions with Naomi and Boaz, she was able to embrace who she was created to be. She recognized the qualities of the servant's heart within her and consequently had no problem telling Boaz, "I am your servant." Ruth had reached a point in her life where she finally embraced who she was without regrets, without fear, and without trying to qualify her accomplishments to feel valued.

QUIET REFLECTIONS _____

So often we judge a person by their outward appearance and fail to look deeper. Samuel nearly made the same mistake when it came time to anoint the second king over Israel. Each son of Jesse that came before him, Samuel thought God would surely want as king. David was ultimately chosen, not because of his looks, or his skill with a slingshot. He was chosen based on the content of his heart. David knew from a young age that he was a worshipper and he was content to be that—even if it meant he only sang in front of a bunch of sheep!

How have the scars you carry affected your hope-seed? Take a moment to reflect on the relationships you have. What have you learned about yourself from each of these relationships? Based on what you have learned, who do you say you are?

_____ **PRAYER TIME**

Father, I thank You for every person You have placed in my life that has helped me better understand who You have designed me to be. Help me to recognize and begin to operate in my untapped potential as I continually uncover the gifts and talents You have given me to steward. Show me any area of my life that is not pleasing to You and cleanse my heart from any unwarranted judgments I have placed on myself. I love You, Lord, and I bless what You are doing in my life. Amen.

YOUR FOOD FOR THOUGHT MOMENT

Are you searching for happiness? One of the keys to true happiness is living authentically. The experts may give you a twelve-step formula to find happiness, but you can still feel empty and unfulfilled.

In Matthew, Jesus talks to us about resting, a seemingly unrelated topic. Let's take a look at what He says.

Come to Me, all you who labor and are heavy laden, and I will give you rest. Take My yoke upon you and learn from Me, for I am gentle and lowly in heart, and you will find rest for your souls (Matthew 11:28-29, NKJV).

Why resting? Because it is in the resting that He speaks to us about who we are and we find His strength. Knowing who you are in Christ is essential to living a hope-filled authentic life.

Here are a few things God says about you.

- He calls you His friend (John 15:14).
- He considers you the apple of His eye (Psalms 17:8).
- He says you are seated with Jesus Christ in heavenly places (Ephesians 2:4-7).
- He calls you God's workmanship created in Christ Jesus (Ephesians 2:10).

Leading an authentic life means being true to yourself—the person you are in Christ. I encourage you to write down your own statements, then begin rehearsing each one, allowing them to rest deep in your heart.

My Personal Reflections

My God Speaks

_____

_____

_____

_____

_____

_____

_____

_____

_____

_____

_____

_____

_____

_____

_____

_____

_____

_____

_____

_____

"The six measures of barley given her by Boaz marked significant turning points in Ruth's life. To begin with, it marked the end of her season of gleaning a living off of what others had sown."

DAY
22

SIX MEASURES OF BARLEY

———— ⚜ ————

So she lay at his feet until morning, and she arose before one could recognize another. Then he said, "Do not let it be known that the woman came to the threshing floor." Also he said, "Bring the shawl that is on you and hold it." And when she held it, he measured six ephahs of barley, and laid it on her. Then she went into the city.

~(Ruth 3:14-15, NKJV)

Before he sends her back home, Boaz tells Ruth to hold out her shawl as he pours into it six measures of barley. The object she used as a covering now becomes a tool to help carry the multiplied provision coming her way. A shawl was seen as commonplace and average, the purpose of which was defined based on the circumstances and the need of the possessor. In Ruth's case, her circumstances were about to take a drastic turn and now her shawl is redefined by her redeemer and it transforms into a means to lay hold of the new thing God was pouring into her life.

She went from handfuls of blessings—the little she could get a grip on in the moment—to an abundance that would cover her completely; something she could wrap herself up in. What would it feel like to be wrapped up in a blessing?

Back on her first day in the field at the beginning of the barley season, Ruth carried home one ephah of barley, which was enough grain to feed her mother-in-law and herself for the next *six days*. Now at the end of the harvest season Boaz lays upon her *six ephahs of barley*. That number is five more than she started out with! God took the little she had in her hand and poured His abundance of grace into it.

The six measures of barley given her by Boaz marked significant turning points in Ruth's life. To begin with, it marked the end of her season of gleaning a living off of what others had sown. It was the end of her days of picking up what others left behind. The gift of six measures also marked the last time she would be seen as poor or a servant of others. Her days of striving and self-preservation were over. No longer would she carry a burden laid upon her by another.

As the morning dawned in the natural, so Ruth's new day began. When she walked away from the threshing floor, she walked into her brand-new season.

QUIET REFLECTIONS _____

What burdens are you carrying that have been placed upon you by someone else? Are there areas in your life where you find yourself striving to survive? To break free? Whose fields have you been gleaning in? Are you feeding on barley (signifying the mindset of poverty and lack), or wheat (signifying the mindset of abundance and prosperity)? Moses carried a staff with him and when his circumstances changed, it transformed into a rod of power to part the Red Sea. What do you have in your hand that can be turned into a tool to assist you in your future?

_____ PRAYER TIME

Father, I thank You that You have provided for my every need by allowing me to glean nuggets of purpose from those You have placed in my life. I thank You for Your sustaining power during my season of famine. And I thank You that You have brought me into a place of unlimited supply. Today I declare and decree that my time of feeding on poverty mindsets is over! From this day forth I shall feed my seed of hope on the abundance of Your provision and Your limitless resources! I love You, and I bless what You are doing in my life. Amen.

My Personal Reflections

_____

_____

_____

_____

_____

_____

_____

_____

_____

_____

_____

_____

_____

_____

_____

_____

_____

My God Speaks

_____

_____

_____

_____

_____

_____

_____

_____

_____

_____

_____

_____

_____

_____

_____

"Waiting on the Lord can be one of the most difficult things a believer is asked to do. Psalms 46:10 encourages us to quiet ourselves and recognize He is God."

DAY
23

BE STILL

Then she said, "Sit still, my daughter, until you know how the matter will turn out; for the man will not rest until he has concluded the matter this day."

~(Ruth 3:18, NKJV)

The law of Moses as recorded in the Old Testament made provisions for widows and the poor. When a woman became a widow her son was to take care of her. However, after the deaths of Mahlon and Chilion, this option was no longer available to Naomi. And Ruth never had children.

The Law went on to say that if the son could not care for his mother, then the brother of the deceased was responsible to marry his widowed sister-in-law and raise up a son on behalf of his brother. Since Naomi and her husband had moved to Moab away from their relatives, there was no family member living nearby who could fulfill this option for her. Nor was this option available to Ruth because her brother-in-law Chilion had also passed away.

The next option available to Ruth was if a blood relative of her husband's family would be willing to pay the price of redemption. This man would be called the kinsman-redeemer and his act of redemption covered much more than marrying the deceased man's widow. It also involved buying back any land that had been sold at the husband's death to pay off any indebtedness. The act of redemption provided by the kinsmen-redeemer was designed to be one of protection, by keeping the property of the deceased within the clan.

This kinsman-redeemer had to be someone who was willing to take on the added responsibility of the marriage, as well as someone with the financial means to manage the additional land or property. The transaction of redemption was most often carried out at the city gate because of the need for witnesses.

Knowing the only option available was the hope of finding a kinsman-redeemer Ruth is offered some poignant advice by Naomi—"Sit still and wait. Your kinsman-redeemer is moving behind the scenes to set things in motion for your complete deliverance. In the meantime, you can't lift a finger to help."

Up until this point, Ruth had been working out her faith every single day by going into her field of opportunity. Now she is instructed not to move, but simply wait and see what God would do. She had already sown her seed of hope throughout the entire barley and wheat harvest seasons. Now she needed to sit back and let her faith work.

Waiting on the Lord can be one of the most difficult things a believer is asked to do. Psalms 46:10 encourages us to quiet ourselves and recognize that He is God. With the instruction to sit still and wait, Ruth could not keep herself in front of Boaz and thereby, could not continually remind him of her need. In fact, she wasn't to speak of her need to him at all. He was already well aware of it. Nor was she to talk to her friends about what was happening, or about what she wanted to happen. All she could do was sit quietly and wait.

Perhaps her silence was to prevent her from defining the new thing God was doing by her own limited beliefs and words. Our words create the container for the next move of God in our lives. We must be careful not to define what He is doing out of our own limited speech. When we instead allow the Holy Spirit to construct the container by giving voice to His inner promptings, we will end up with a structure that can truly support the new thing God is bringing to pass.

QUIET REFLECTIONS _____

An ancient Christian exercise known as contemplative prayer was practiced by, among others, Bernard of Clairvaux, a 12th-century monk. In essence, it is a type of prayer that has at its foundation three guiding principles—listen, watch, and wait. Madame Jeanne Guyon, a French Christian mystic from the late 17th and early 18th centuries, and an advocate of contemplative prayer, suggested the best way to quiet the heart and soul was to meditate upon a Scripture verse. How can you incorporate the practice of contemplative prayer into your quiet time with the Lord? What are you listening for?

_____ **PRAYER TIME**

Father, I thank You that You are working all things out for my good and Your glory. As I sit in Your presence I ask that You open my heart to hear Your voice, and open my eyes to see the new thing You are doing. I love You, Lord, and I bless what You are doing in my life. Amen.

YOUR FOOD FOR THOUGHT MOMENT

Bob Sorge, in his book *Secrets of the Secret Place*, says, "Everything in the kingdom depends upon whether or not we hear the word of God."[1]

One of the biggest lies of Satan is that we can't hear the voice of God. However, John 10:27 tells us this is just a ploy of the enemy to keep us out of the secret place. *"My sheep hear my voice."*

To hear His voice requires *listening by waiting.* Check out these verses regarding waiting on the Lord.

Our soul waiteth for the LORD: he is our help and our shield (Psalms 33:20).

Truly my soul waiteth upon God: from him cometh my salvation. He only is my rock and my salvation; he is my defense; I shall not be greatly moved (Psalms 62:1-2).

As we wait before the Lord, He changes our hearts and circumstances to prepare us for the place of influence He has for us. Waiting on the Lord is not an easy discipline to learn, but is perhaps the most powerful tool in the saint's arsenal.

Nothing in the kingdom happens without a word. Every word of God heard and acted upon will bring the change it was intended to bring. God's Word will not return void; it will accomplish everything it was sent to do! Ultimately, the key to change is listening for His voice.

---

[1] Bob Sorge, Secrets of the Secret Place (Greenwood: Oasis House, 2001), 11.

My Personal Reflections

_____

_____

_____

_____

_____

_____

_____

_____

_____

_____

_____

_____

_____

_____

My God Speaks

_____

_____

_____

_____

_____

_____

_____

_____

_____

_____

_____

_____

_____

_____

_____

"Blessing is a form of communicating by giving voice to what is being spoken in heaven. The spoken blessing is a powerful tool in the hand of the believer. It carries the power to awaken gifts, skills, and talents that may be lying dormant within us, and to set the course of the future."

DAY
24

SPOKEN BLESSINGS

And all the people who were at the gate, and the elders, said, "We are witnesses. The LORD make the woman who is coming to your house like Rachel and Leah, the two who built the house of Israel; and may you prosper in Ephrathah and be famous in Bethlehem. May your house be like the house of Perez, whom Tamar bore to Judah, because of the offspring which the LORD will give you from this young woman."

~(Ruth 4:11-12, NKJV)

Boaz completed the transaction necessary to acquire the property of Mahlon and for the redemption of Ruth. Now those gathered there joined in the joyous celebration by immediately pronouncing a blessing on Ruth. They ask God to make her as Rachel and Leah, who together birthed the future leaders of the twelve tribes of the nation of Israel.

They also spoke blessings over the future house of Boaz and Ruth asking that God make it like the house of Perez, the son of Tamar and Judah; their relationship representing another time when the law of Moses was enacted and a son was raised up on behalf of the deceased husband. Judah's first two sons died because of God's judgment on their wickedness. It would seem the third-born son Shelah would then become the natural heir to the tribe of Judah. In fact, he did not. It is Perez, whose name means "breakthrough", (birthed through what some would call unfavorable circumstances) that becomes the head of the tribe and a foundational stone in God's plan for the nation. His name is listed in the lineage of Christ found in the book of Matthew.

Blessing is a form of communicating by giving voice to what is being spoken in heaven. The spoken blessing is a powerful tool in the hand of the believer. It carries the power to awaken gifts, skills, and talents that may be lying dormant within us, and to set the course of the future. Blessing is tied to seeing—peering into something with understanding and wisdom and then putting into words the insight gained. It requires the ability to see circumstances from Christ's perspective.

QUIET REFLECTIONS _____

At the baptism of Jesus as recorded in Mark 1:11, the Father spoke a blessing from heaven over Jesus, declaring Him to be a Son in whom He was well pleased. This affirmation transpired before Jesus began His earthly ministry and confirmed Him as being sent from the Father.

Blessings can come in the form of prophetic utterances. Take time to reflect on the things that people have spoken to you that relate to who you are as a person and what you feel is your destiny. How have the words they spoke affirmed you? Strengthened you? Confirmed your calling? Have any words hindered you and kept you from moving out in faith?

_____ **PRAYER TIME**

Heavenly Father, open my eyes and my heart in this moment to the words that have been spoken as blessings over my life. Show me the way You have used them to sharpen my destiny for my good and Your glory. I thank You that You speak words of life over me each day and I now receive Your spoken blessing over me and thank You for Your affirmation. I love You, Lord, and I bless what You are doing in my life. Amen.

My Personal Reflections

My God Speaks

_____

_____

_____

_____

_____

_____

_____

_____

_____

_____

_____

_____

_____

_____

_____

_____

_____

_____

"Hope is the connecting point between faith and love. This is why the enemy so often tries to attack our sense of hope, even our resolve to be hope-filled, because diminished hope means diminished faith..."

DAY
25

WHAT HOPE NEEDS

So Boaz took Ruth and she became his wife; and when he went in to her, the LORD gave her conception, and she bore a son.

~(Ruth 4:13, NKJV)

A baby arrives not long after Boaz and Ruth marry. Her first marriage produced no children, but now we find Ruth, or "friendship" (the Hebrew meaning of her name), united with Boaz, whose name means "strength, power, might, or flowing." The seed of hope carried by Ruth brought her into the place of redemption and positioned her to find the ultimate fulfillment for the hope she carried—the birth of the next generation.

The flow of power coming through the act of redemption is exactly what Ruth's seed of hope needed. It is the same power available to every open heart when we allow Christ to be our kinsman-redeemer and buy us back from the life of sin.

God waited to give a child to Ruth until the seed of hope she carried could connect to the powerful flow it needed to birth God's intention in their lives. It is the connection between relationship and the flow of power that gives birth to the next move of God, whether that moving occurs within a single heart or within the heart of a nation. It is a kingdom principal that intimacy and power are intertwined. Where there is intimacy with Jesus you will also find power to do and be all He has said. The flow of heaven is looking for a friend on Earth to unite with and thereby release His power, His glory, His revelation, His strength.

Hope is the connecting point between faith and love. This is why the enemy so often tries to attack our sense of hope, even our resolve to be hope-filled, because diminished hope means diminished faith, and diminished faith will weaken our love for one another and for God.

QUIET REFLECTIONS _____

Acts 9:11-19 is the account of Ananias coming to Saul following his conversion on the Damascus road. Because of all the persecution Saul had rendered against Christians, the Lord had to speak to Ananias twice before he obeyed. Ananias could have stopped a great outpouring of God in that generation and in future generations because of the level of fear and mistrust he carried. Ultimately, he had to let go of his fear and allow his hope to bring him into a place of faith that God was up to something good, and a place where he could reach out to Saul in love, even to the point of addressing him as "brother" when they met.

What are you hoping for in this season of your life? How is it tied to your faith for what God is wanting to do in you, and through you? Describe your love walk. Can you get along with most people, or are there areas and situations where you are holding grudges, and unforgiveness?

_____ PRAYER TIME

Heavenly Father, I thank You for Your blessing of new life for this day. And I thank You that You are bringing me to a place where my hope, faith, and love are strong and working together with Your power to release revival in my heart and in the hearts and lives of those I touch. I love You, Lord, and I bless what You are doing in my life. Amen.

My Personal Reflections

_____

_____

_____

_____

_____

_____

_____

_____

_____

_____

_____

_____

_____

_____

_____

_____

_____

My God Speaks

_____

_____

_____

_____

_____

_____

_____

_____

_____

_____

_____

_____

_____

_____

_____

"God had a plan for Naomi's life. In His providence, He restores to Naomi her own flow. Her body was no longer producing milk however, God changed the laws of nature and allowed milk to come from a woman outside the age of bearing children."

DAY
26

NAOMI'S RESTORATION

Then the women said to Naomi, "Blessed be the LORD, who has not left you this day without a close relative; and may his name be famous in Israel! And may he be to you a restorer of life and a nourisher of your old age; for your daughter-in-law, who loves you, who is better to you than seven sons, has borne him." Then Naomi took the child and laid him on her bosom, and became a nurse to him.

~(Ruth 4:14-16, NKJV)

God didn't stop with the redemption of Ruth. Now that He had these two woman tied together, He could not release one without releasing the other. He had to make sure Naomi was in on what He was doing as well.

Remember, this is the same Naomi who said of herself, "I went out full and came back empty"; the same woman who told others to call her Bitter, for she saw her own pleasantness drained from her. She believed life had passed her by. At the beginning of her story she carried hope that she still had a future in God's economy. After ten years in Moab every ounce of life was drained from her hope-seed and it lay as dry as a rose petal pressed between the pages of a book.

But now, ten years later, she is standing once again in Bethlehem holding in her arms the realization of the hope she thought was dead and gone. Moab brought her to a point where she had stopped dreaming about legacy and future generations, believing that part of her life was over. Now, she is not only holding her grandson, but is the one chosen to be his nurse.

God had a plan for Naomi's life. In His providence, He restores to Naomi her own flow. Her body was no longer producing milk however, God changed the laws of nature and allowed milk to come from a woman outside the age of bearing children. His plan of restoration for Naomi removed every ounce of bitterness built up in her body that blocked her ability to flow with His plans.

Because Naomi allowed her seed of hope to flourish again, and allowed someone else to connect to that seed of hope who at the time was hurting just as much as she was, God gave her a part to play in the powerful flow unleashed by the union of Ruth and Boaz at the beginning of the unfolding story of His Seed of Hope.

This "new thing" God was doing was yet in its infancy. Infants need pure milk to feed upon; it cannot be tainted in any form if the child is to grow and develop in a healthy way. God put a woman in charge of feeding His "new thing" only after bitterness had been completely removed from her. Now that her seed of hope has been brought into its own fullness, Naomi can set about letting it be the source of sustenance and strength for the next generation nursing at her breast.

QUIET REFLECTIONS _____

What are the sources you are "feeding" on? How is God using them to develop your character? Your faith? Your love? Who is feeding on what you carry? Legacy is not always about the ability to have children in the natural. It is more about the power to birth sons and daughters in the kingdom. Take some time now to meditate on your legacy and write down the dreams you carry for it and the future God has for you.

_____ **PRAYER TIME**

Father, I thank You that You have given and continue to give me a legacy. I thank You that as I sit before You now, You are revealing to me the ways I am leaving a legacy for my natural children and my spiritual sons and daughters. Show me how to impact their lives in such a way as to release Your glory and power to them and through them, and to advance Your kingdom on Earth. I love You, Lord, and I bless what You are doing in my life. Amen.

My Personal Reflections

_____

_____

_____

_____

_____

_____

_____

_____

_____

_____

_____

_____

_____

_____

My God Speaks

_____

_____

_____

_____

_____

_____

_____

_____

_____

_____

_____

_____

_____

_____

_____

_____

_____

"Boaz continues on in both the roles of his predecessors as he becomes the kinsman-redeemer to Ruth. He symbolically is a type of Christ who leads his people out of bondage, and confirms the covenant between God and man."

DAY
27

WHAT'S IN THE FAMILY LINE?

Also the neighbor women gave him a name, saying, "There is a son born to Naomi." And they called his name Obed. He is the father of Jesse, the father of David.

~(Ruth 4:17, NKJV)

Naomi's heritage had not been cut off or taken from her with the death of her own sons. We see the restoration of Naomi coming full circle with the birth of her grandson. The women gathered around Ruth and Naomi are the ones who name the baby. Sometimes those around us can see things that we may have a limited perspective on. In this case, they named the baby based on the character they saw reflected in Ruth through her treatment and care of Naomi.

It is clear throughout the story that Ruth's connection to Naomi was one of service born out of love. She could have walked away many times since they left Moab, going back on her promise to stay with Naomi and allowing her people and religious beliefs to become her own. Keeping her word to her mother-in-law had such an impact on how the people of the community saw Ruth that they suggested a name that has "servant" as one of its meanings.

Obed, like any other child, carried in his blood the DNA from both his parents. Ruth's DNA as a Moabitess—one birthed out of a sense of failed fatherhood—was transformed into that of an Israelite, the seed of God. The restructuring of her DNA came about because of her decision to follow the God of Israel. Each day as she went about her daily activities she became more and more familiar with the will and the ways of her new God. Each day the awareness of her brokenness and aloneness were transformed into an awareness of God's provision and tender care. Any lingering effects in her spirit caused by failed fatherhood were swept away by the goodness of a loving Father.

This newborn son also carried a powerful DNA from his father, Boaz. It is the lineage of Boaz that forms the foundation of the family line—a foundation that had to be one of great strength, for out of it would come the future king of Israel.

Boaz was the grandson of Nahshon, who was one of the princes in the nation of Israel. In fact, he was the leader of the tribe of Judah during the time of Moses. Nahshon, as the tribal leader, was positioned at the head of Judah's encampment around the tabernacle.

As the Israelites moved from camp to camp in the wilderness, it was the tribe of Judah that led out first, again with Nahshon at the point. Here in this first position Nahshon symbolically is seen as a type of Christ who leads His people out from their bondage.

Nahshon operated under the leadership of Moses, whom God had appointed as deliverer to Israel. The tribe of Judah represented the worshippers, or the people of praise. In his role of symbolically representing Christ, Nahshon was leading the people of praise out of their bondage. It is the one who praises that can move forward into their promised land and all that God has for them.

Nahshon had a son named Salma, or Salmon. It was Salmon that took over the leadership of Judah and led them into the land of Canaan. Salmon's name has as one of its meanings "the act of establishing in office, or ratifying." Salmon serves as one who ratifies, or confirms the covenant between God and Israel by leading the tribe of Judah out of the wilderness and into the Promised Land. Salmon, the confirmer of the covenant, later became the father of Boaz. Boaz continues on in both the roles of his predecessors as he becomes the kinsman-redeemer to Ruth. He symbolically is a type of Christ who leads his people out of bondage, and confirms the covenant between God and man.

Obed is set up by God to be born into a family of servants, leaders, and covenant keepers. In him, the lineage of his ancestors merge into one, so that through him a future king is born.

QUIET REFLECTIONS _____

You may have a power-packed family line just as Boaz did. Or you may have a heritage like that of Ruth. Regardless, as believers we all have a great line of predecessors in the faith. Take time to review your heritage as a child of God found in Hebrews 11, paying close attention to the character and nature of faith each person named brings into the family line.

_____ **PRAYER TIME**

Father, I thank You that You confirmed Your covenant with me when You sent Your Son to die in my place. I thank You that You are a covenant-keeping God. You will never waver or shy away from Your love for me. Father, I ask that You show me the power of keeping covenant with those around me. Reveal to me Your will and teach me Your ways, O God. Father, I love You, and I bless what You are doing in my life. Amen.

YOUR FOOD FOR THOUGHT MOMENT

Have you ever checked your genealogy? Learning who we are and where we come from can give us perspective and a sense of heritage. Did you know you have a liar, a murderer, world changers, national leaders, and a friend of God in your family line?

It's easy to see how God can use world changers and national leaders. It's a little more difficult to see how He can use the more ordinary, average person. And yet He does every single day.

Noah became a world changer when God used him to bring about a new start for all of humanity. Why Noah? Because God considered him righteous and blameless in his generation. Abraham lied to Pharaoh saying Sarah was his sister when Pharaoh took her for himself. However, God chose to focus on Abraham's obedience and willingness to faithfully follow His direction. Moses killed an Egyptian and then lived on the run for the next forty years. But God considered him a friend; one that He would speak to face to face.

When you hit moments of second-guessing yourself, of fear instead of faith, moments when the pain seems greater than the reward, remember you have a long history of faithful followers of God in your family line. He chooses to work with us through our weaknesses to display His strength and power.

My Personal Reflections

_____

_____

_____

_____

_____

_____

_____

_____

_____

_____

_____

_____

_____

_____

_____

_____

_____

My God Speaks

_____

_____

_____

_____

_____

_____

_____

_____

_____

_____

_____

_____

_____

_____

_____

_____

_____

_____

_____

"Pure worship needs a place to be birthed,

a place of settled hope where it can grow

in freedom and have a lasting impact. True

worship says, 'There is no other spirit that

will rule over my life but

the Spirit of the Almighty God.'"

DAY
28

BIRTHING WORSHIP

---

*Give unto the LORD the glory due to His name; worship the
LORD in the beauty of holiness.*

~(Psalms 29:2, NKJV)

As we have seen, Obed was born into a family line of covenant keepers and redeemers. As the firstborn son, he would continue building the family name, or rather he would add to the foundation already laid by his fore-fathers. We also know one of the meanings for the name Obed is "servant." We see the essence of who Ruth proclaimed herself to be now carried forward into her son. "I'm your maidservant, she declared, when first questioned by Boaz in the field. In fact, it was Ruth's servant heart that nurtured her seed of hope throughout her journey, so when the time came for the seed to produce what naturally came forth was a servant.

There is another meaning to the name Obed and that is "worshipper." This son would be one whose very service was an act of worship. The lineage God wanted to bring about could only be produced through the union of Strength (Boaz) and Friendship (Ruth). It is the union of Power and Friendship that produces worship—God's power bound together in unity with our friendship with Him.

Boaz was already a man of wealth with land and servants, and he was a community leader. Now he finally has what he has wanted, the one thing that has been missing in his life up to this point. With the birth of Obed, the Worshipping Servant, came the son who would carry the legacy forward from his great grandfather, and in fact the past seven generations.

Obed was the eighth son in the family line. The number eight represents new beginnings or coming full circle. With his birth came a new beginning in both Boaz and Ruth's lives. When worship is birthed in your life your new beginning will come too.

Praising and worshipping God is the best way to open a door for Him to step through. It not only gives God access to the earthly arena, but it gives the worshipper access to heaven. Adoring our Lord in worship gives Him permission to act on our behalf, and it is the place where He grants us permission to act as His agents in the earth.

Ruth let go of all her past belief systems and put herself in line with God's plan to connect with her kinsman-redeemer. In so doing, the son of worship had a legitimate birth. The distinction between legitimate worship and illegitimate is this—the one is based on a right relationship with our redeemer, Jesus Christ, and the other is based on self-effort and self-promotion.

God had to turn Naomi's captivity and remove every ounce of bitterness from her, because worship cannot feed on bitterness and survive. Bitterness cannot be commingled with the sweet incense of pure worship, for it will cause our prayers to be tainted with self-centered, ego-driven desires, ultimately giving off a putrid scent of decay and hindering the blessing of heaven.

Pure worship needs a place to be birthed, a place of settled hope where it can grow in freedom and have a lasting impact. True worship says, 'There is no other spirit that will rule over my life but the Spirit of the Almighty God.'" Worship announces to the enemy that our trust is in the Living God!

QUIET REFLECTIONS _____

Deep within the heart of a worshipper lies the seed of hope. As a worshipper, you carry hope for the realization of God's plans on Earth. Do you believe that your worship creates a pathway for the glory of God to move and invites the intervention of heaven into seemingly unchangeable situations? Will understanding that your worship carries the power to affect situations and circumstances change the way you worship? Worship can take many forms but all require the basic ingredient of obedience. Are you walking in obedience to the Word of God? What are some of the ways you worship God?

_____ **PRAYER TIME**

Father, I thank You that You are the God of all hope. In You I found all my desire and all my strength. You are a great and mighty God and beside You there is none. You are awesome in all Your ways and fearful in Your praises. I exalt Your name above every situation and circumstance I face this day. I give You praise and honor because You are a good and faithful Father. I trust that You are working all things together for my good and Your glory. I love You, Lord, and I bless what You are doing in my life. Amen.

YOUR FOOD FOR THOUGHT MOMENT

Have you ever thought about the impact your worship can have? Often we think our greater impact to bring change is through the power of our prayers. While the impact of prayer cannot be negated, the impact of our worship is just as powerful.

John 4:23-24 tells us God is looking for people who will worship Him in spirit and truth. In spirit means with our whole heart engaged, completely surrendering our spirit to the influence of the Holy Spirit and allowing Him to direct our interaction with the Father. To worship in truth means to have a singleness of heart to focus on God as the person of our worship.

Allow me to pose a question to you. If you truly believed your worship could affect your nation, how would you worship differently? Would you spend more time in worship and less time in bringing your requests before the Lord? Would you focus time each day on acknowledging who He is and recognizing His authority over all things? Would you speak of His greatness more and your needs less?

Ralph Waldo Emerson once said, "What greater calamity can fall upon a nation than the loss of worship?"[2] Oh that we may see our worship as the change agent needed in our nation and seek to make it a focus of our heart!

---

[2] Ralph Waldo Emerson, "Divinity School Address" (lecture, Divinity College, Cambridge, July 15, 1838).

My Personal Reflections

My God Speaks

"David had plenty of opportunity to allow

bitterness to enter back into his worship...

Instead, his worship was honest and pure,

coming straight from the heart of someone

deeply in love with God."

DAY

29

WHERE WILL WORSHIP CARRY YOU?

And in that day there shall be a Root of Jesse, who shall stand as a banner to the people; for the Gentiles shall seek Him, and His resting place shall be glorious.

~(Isaiah 11:10, NKJV)

Through the redemption given her by Boaz, Ruth was an accepted member of society, and because of it she had the right to hope for the same thing that other Israelite women dreamed of having a part in. She turned her hope seed loose to dream of being the one chosen to birth the Messiah. Her son Obed, the Worshiping-Servant, later becomes the father of Jesse, who in turn, becomes the father of David, the second king of Israel.

Jesse's name means "extant, or currently existing." His life was lived in the present moment, the here and now. Right here, right now God is moving! It's hard to see sometimes when there is so much negativity happening around us, but the fact holds true. God is moving in your life in the present moment. Jesse represents the one who makes a mark in the present that will affect future generations.

There are some stunning prophecies in the Old Testament regarding Jesse so you would think he would be a noteworthy powerhouse for God. Actually, his real claim to fame was that he was the link between the birth of worship and the outcome of what worship produced. He is the bridge between the birth of worship and the establishment of the kingdom where worship is taken to the next level.

Jesse seemed to be a typical business man of his day. He owned land and livestock and his sons helped in the family business. One day the prophet Samuel arrived in Bethlehem with the intent to anoint the next king of Israel. Samuel invites Jesse and his sons to the feast he was hosting, but Jesse only brings seven of his sons, leaving David at home to care for the sheep.

Perhaps his decision to leave David behind was based on the need of the moment. Someone needed to watch the sheep and since David was the youngest, Jesse picked him. Perhaps it rested in Jesse's belief that God could not use David. Perhaps he didn't want David around because he reminded him of his past sin and failure. David does record for us in Psalms 51 these poignant words, "in sin my mother conceived me."

Looking back at the family history we can see the seed of failed fatherhood trying to resurface through Jesse. Ruth's seed of hope overcame the history of failed fatherhood within her own generation. However, the imprint of failed fatherhood still lingered on the seed and tried to resurrect again through Jesse and move into future generations. God had to directly intervene through the prophet Samuel to stop the seed of hope from growing in the wrong direction and producing a tree that was so distorted it would need to be cut down, forcing God to start over again with a different selection for king.

If God had left the decision of kingship up to Jesse that day he would have picked one of the other boys. From his viewpoint his older sons were smarter, well liked, and all-around better choices for God to use. If Jesse's expectations for David were low, then David could never use his father's hope seed as a source of nourishment for his own seed of hope. David had to learn to feed his seed from other sources.

David had plenty of opportunity to allow bitterness to enter back into his worship. He certainly had plenty of chances to be angry and resentful, but he never let any of it take root in his heart. Instead, his worship was honest and pure, coming straight from the heart of someone deeply in love with God.

QUIET REFLECTIONS _____

The story of David's anointing is told in First Samuel 16. Samuel consecrates Jesse and his sons so they can partake in the feast. However, when David appears before him, he doesn't take time to consecrate him before the Lord. He simply pours the anointing oil over him. David appears before Samuel in his marketplace role carrying on the family business. God did not require him to remove his "business" garments before anointing him for his upcoming role as king. David allowed his worship to carry him from his present circumstances into his future.

Besides being a worshipper, what do you carry an anointing for? Where will you allow your worship to carry you? Where do you see yourself in five years? Ten years?

_____ **PRAYER TIME**

Father, I thank You for the deposit of hope You have placed in my life. Father, Your Word tell us that You are looking for worshippers who will worship in spirit and truth. I ask You, Holy Spirit, to teach me how to pour out my alabaster box in worship. Show me Lord, how to mine the depths of adoration and praise as You reveal Your goodness to me more and more. Show me those things You have planned for my future and teach me how to walk into them. I love You, Lord, and I bless what You are doing in my life. Amen.

YOUR FOOD FOR THOUGHT MOMENT

Calvin Coolidge is quoted as saying, "It is only when men begin to worship that they begin to grow."[3] I immediately had to ask myself, how am I growing through my worship?

It's during times of worship that we encounter the nature of God and He pours into us of Himself. Worship is the place I become more like Jesus. It's the place where I exchange my pain for His healing, release my sorrow for His joy, and let go of my bondage to take on His yoke. Worship is where His nature of peace overtakes my anger and frustration, where His nature of love overtakes my fears.

Jehoshaphat, when surrounded by three armies, first sent the worshippers into battle. They overcame by declaring two simple phrases: "Praise the Lord, for His mercy endures forever." (See 2 Chronicles 20.)

Herein lies a foundational principal as it relates to spiritual warfare. *In order to say, you must first see. In order to see, you must first worship. Worship precedes seeing, seeing precedes saying.*

Our ability to see into the spiritual realm comes out of a place of worship. Jesus said of Himself, "I *speak* that which I have *seen* with my Father." (See John 8:38.) Once we *see* what God is up to, we can begin to *say* what He is saying and do what He is doing.

---

[3]Calvin Coolidge. BrainyQuote.com, Xplore Inc, 2016. http://www.brainyquote.com/quotes/quotes/c/calvincool397166.html, accessed June 22, 2016.

My Personal Reflections

_____

_____

_____

_____

_____

_____

_____

_____

_____

_____

_____

_____

_____

_____

_____

_____

_____

_____

My God Speaks

_____

_____

_____

_____

_____

_____

_____

_____

_____

_____

_____

_____

_____

_____

_____

_____

_____

"When we allow our own seed of hope to be broken open as Ruth allowed hers to be, we will find the image of the King of Glory contained within."

DAY
30

MAKE ROOM FOR A KING

***

There shall come forth a Rod from the stem of Jesse, and a Branch shall grow out of his roots. The Spirit of the LORD shall rest upon Him, the Spirit of wisdom and understanding, the Spirit of counsel and might, the Spirit of knowledge and of the fear of the LORD.

~(Isaiah 11:1-2, NKJV)

Out of the loins of Obed, the Worshipping Servant, comes David, the Worshipping Warrior-King. Buried within the tiny crevices of Ruth's seed of hope was the image of a king.

While Jesse, as David's father, failed to see the greatness contained within the young man before him, God looked on the heart of David and saw the image of the king carried in the seed. And then He set in motion a plan to bring that seed to the forefront of the family line.

David was well known for his ability to worship. While out in the fields watching sheep, he would write songs of praise and worship. His gift of worship was a tremendous source that nourished David's hope seed. When Saul, the first king of Israel, needed a musician to help calm his troubled spirit, he sent for David. Eventually he asks that David be allowed to come live in the palace with him. It was David's heart of worship that first carried him into the palace, not Samuel's anointing as the future king of Israel.

Later, when Saul knew that God had snatched the kingdom from him and intended to give it to David, he set out to kill him. During the season of battle, there were many opportunities for David to lose sight of the benefits of being a worshipper and many opportunities for him to lash out at Saul with the same hatred and anger he was employing against David.

But David had learned the habit of nurturing his seed of hope through fellowship with God. He would take himself to a quiet place where he could talk with God one on one, and God answered with hope.

David is so enthralled with worshipping God that when he does become king and the Ark of the Covenant is captured by the Philistines, he works to bring it back to the nation of Israel. When it finally arrives, he does not return it to the site where the Tabernacle of Moses was located. Instead, he sets it up on a hill where anyone could come directly into the Presence of God to worship, then sets in place divisions of musicians and singers to worship the Lord around the clock. In David's tent there was no place for blood sacrifices or ceremonial washings carried out by the priesthood. There was only the sacrifice of worship and the cleansing of the heart by the power of praise for all who entered there.

God carefully continues to form the image of His future king, encoding it into the bloodlines of Boaz and Ruth, and passing it down from generation to generation until the seed finds its way into a young girl named Mary.

The Son born of Mary was known as the Branch that would come out of the root of Jesse spoken about by the prophet Isaiah. He would grow up in the pattern of David and would be the ultimate realization of the family heritage of Worshiping Servant, Worshiping Warrior, and Worshiping King combined in one. This Son is the fulfillment of fourteen generations of hope-seeds. He is Jesus Christ, the Hope of Glory.

When we allow our own seed of hope to be broken open as Ruth allowed hers to be, we will find the image of the King of Glory contained within. The desire to be like our Papa, our Father God, to be the replica of His image here on Earth, is at the core of our seed of hope.

Every seed produces after its own kind. An apple seed will not give you an oak tree. It will grow into an apple tree, which in turn will bear fruit and give you apples. Every seed produces what is encoded within its core.

When we allow the Hope of Glory room in our hearts, He will be the nurturing force to our seed of hope, growing it into a powerful fruit-bearing tree that replicates His image on Earth and is capable of giving life to others.

QUIET REFLECTIONS _____

God released His seed of Hope, Jesus, to reach those broken down by circumstances and brokenhearted from despair. The Father chose from eternity past just who He wanted in the family line for His Seed of Hope. His choice started long before Mary, the mother of Jesus, was ever born. He chose people who on the surface didn't look like much. They were people who made mistakes, people who had issues from their past, people who struggled with who they were called to be and where they fit in in life. But He held fast to His choices and nurtured the seed of hope within each of them until they became what He designed them to be all along.

All He asked of them was to let Him be their guide on the journey. It is the same thing He asks of us today. If you will allow His Seed of Hope, the Hope of Glory, to touch your seed, you will discover a life of adventure and boundless hope waiting for you. Let the adventure begin!

_____ PRAYER TIME

Father, I thank You for the journey of hope You have brought me on. I thank You for leading me through the tough times when my hope-seed was battered by defeat and overwhelmed by circumstances. I thank You for the way You continued to nourish me with Your love and Your Word. Holy Spirit, I ask that You would reveal Jesus to me more and more as I yield to Your leading. May the realization of the Hope of Glory, Christ in me, be my daily bread. I love You, Lord, and I bless what You are doing in my life. Amen.

My Personal Reflections

My God Speaks

_____

_____

_____

_____

_____

_____

_____

_____

_____

_____

_____

_____

_____

_____

_____

_____

_____

_____

MEET THE AUTHOR

Brenda Fink has been active in ministry for 30 years, using her gifts as a Christian Education Director, Elder, Speaker, and Teacher. She has a strong desire to see the body of Christ moving in their kingdom mandate to bring about the fulfillment of Habakkuk 2:14, the Glory of the Lord covering the earth. Brenda is the Founder and President of GloryReleasers ministry, based in Orlando, Florida. GloryReleasers is an organization dedicated to deepening the awareness of God's presence in the earth through writing, teaching, and hands-on ministry.

She loves to inspire people to:

*Uncover their hidden potential
*Increase their effectiveness
*Become intentional influencers

Brenda lives in Orlando, Florida, where she attends Church on the Living Edge. She welcomes comments at GloryReleasers.com or GloryReleasers@yahoo.com.

CONTACT THE AUTHOR

Please email or write the author with any comments you may have. You are also welcome to contact her for bookings. As the Holy Spirit leads, Brenda is available for book club presentations, book signings, or speaking engagements for your church or organization (women's ministries, women's clubs, conferences, workshops, retreats, and seminars). She is available for ministerial and business presentations, each developed specifically for your group or event.

Contact her at:

GloryReleasers@yahoo.com

www.twitter.com/Brenda Fink

www.facebook.com/Brenda Fink

For bookings visit:

www.GloryReleasers.com

or GloryReleasers@yahoo.com

MORE FROM THE AUTHOR

Do you have a hunger for a deeper understanding of truth that cannot be satisfied? Or a thirst that cannot be quenched? *Mysteries of the Dark: Delving into the Hidden Treasures of the Secret Place* is for those who live their everyday lives with a kingdom mindset.

Within its pages you will:

*Uncover the treasure hidden within your heart
*Experience the passion of the Father's heartbeat
*Understand God's plan for kingdom expansion
*See the unfolding realization of God's Glory in the earth
*Know the depth of God's love for you

Mysteries of the Dark: Delving into the Hidden Treasures of the Secret Place is written with simple but profound words that will move the reader deeper into the Throne Room and the Presence of the King.

Order your copy today! Available at:
www.GloryReleasers.com
www.amazon.com and other fine book retailers
Just ask for the book.

www.ingramcontent.com/pod-product-compliance
Lightning Source LLC
LaVergne TN
LVHW051512080426
835509LV00017B/2033